# You're Not *the* Only One

## *Learning How to Handle Emotional Overload*

# You're Not *the* Only One

***Learning How to Handle Emotional Overload***

***Tami Coble Brown***

Published by Gospel Advocate Co.
1006 Elm Hill Pike, Nashville, TN 37210
www.gospeladvocate.com

ISBN: 978-0-89225-663-1

# DEDICATION

*To three women who have always been a positive influence in my life:*

*my mom, Hazel Coble,*
*and my two sisters,*
*Carole English and Lynne Adams*

*Table of*

# CONTENTS

# INTRODUCTION

Have you ever felt so depressed that even simple daily tasks seemed difficult? You're not the only one. I know a girl who was so unhappy with her circumstances that she cried all the time and stopped eating.

Have you ever been so angry that you seriously wanted to hurt someone? You're not the only one. I know a man who had to move far away from home because of death threats from his own brother, who was angry at something that he did.

Have you ever been so afraid that you were literally paralyzed? You're not the only one. I know a ruler and military leader who was so frightened by some news that he heard, he lay on the ground and had no strength.

Actually, I don't know these people personally. I know them from reading about them in the Bible. Hannah, the mother of Samuel, was the girl who stopped eating (1 Samuel 1:7). Jacob was the man who had to leave home because his brother, Esau, wanted to kill him (Genesis 27:42-44). And King Saul was the leader who had no strength when he heard that he and his sons would be killed in battle (1 Samuel 28:19-20). Though many things have changed since those ancient times, one thing has not changed. We all struggle at times with depression, anger and fear, along with many other negative emotions and habits.

You can go to any bookstore or library and find a whole section of self-help books written by doctors, psychologists, counselors and therapists giving their professional advice on how to improve your life. You probably have in your home one of the best psychology books ever written – the Bible! Who else could know and understand our greatest needs and desires but God, the great Physician and Creator of all our emotions? God's Word is full of advice and comfort for our longing souls.

Many of the great heroes of the Bible had to learn to deal with negative feelings. Moses, the great lawgiver and respected leader of the Israelites, struggled with fear and low self-esteem. David, who was described as a "man after God's own heart" suffered the pain of guilt and sin in his life. As you read the stories of these and other men and women of the Bible, you can see how God helped them to overcome their emotional barriers and become the great leaders that they were meant to be. Are you feeling overwhelmed by your own fears and frustrations? You're not the only one! Let's see what the Bible has to say on how to handle emotional overload.

Chapter 1

# All the Lonely People

## *Loneliness*

In their classic song "Eleanor Rigby" the Beatles asked the questions, "All the lonely people, where do they all come from? All the lonely people, where do they all belong?" The answer is simple. Lonely people are everywhere, and they come from all walks of life – from the homeless person on the street to the rich widow living alone in her mansion. Loneliness is the new kid at school who just moved to town and doesn't know anybody yet, the young mother who stays at home all day with preschoolers, the newly divorced or widowed person who is trying to adjust to the single life once again, the military spouse whose husband or wife is far away in another country fighting for our freedom, and the elderly person who watches longingly out the window for visitors who seldom come.

You don't even have to be alone to be lonely. You can be at a party or at work or even sitting in a church pew and feel as if you don't have a friend in the world. You're on the outside looking in. Nothing is worse than feeling alone in a crowd. So where do all these lonely people come from? It all started with Adam.

### It Is Not Good for Man to Be Alone

On the sixth day of creation, God made all the animals, creeping things and beasts. He also created Adam. "Then the LORD God took the man and put him in the Garden of Eden to tend and keep it" (Genesis 2:15). At that point, Adam was all alone in the Garden. In Genesis 1:31, we read that God looked at all of His creation and saw that it was very good, but one thing He made was *not* good. God declared in Genesis 2:18, "It is not good that man should be alone; I will make him a helper comparable to him."

God did not make the new helper right away. First, He gave Adam the job of naming all the animals. Genesis 2:20 says, "So Adam gave names to all the cattle, to the birds of the air, and to every beast of the field. But for Adam there was not found a helper comparable to him." Adam must have noticed there were two of every animal but only one of him. Why did God do this? He allowed Adam to experience loneliness to make him realize that he needed a companion. God saved His best creation for last. He fashioned a woman out of one of Adam's ribs and presented her to the man. Adam was delighted when he met his new companion saying, "This is now bone of my bones and flesh of my flesh" (v. 23).

God instituted marriage and family as a way to alleviate loneliness. He created us with an innate need for love and companionship. When Jesus was asked a question about divorce, He quoted from Genesis: "Have you not read that He who made them at the beginning 'made them male and female,' and said, 'For this reason, a man shall leave his father and mother and be joined to his wife and the two shall become one flesh'?" Jesus then added, "So then, they are no longer two but one flesh. Therefore what God has joined together, let not man separate" (Matthew 19:4-6).

Jesus clearly showed that marriage was between a man and a woman, not two men or two women. He also emphasized that marriage was to be a special and sacred bond. It was to be a relationship held in honor, not something to be thrown away when conflict arises. Paul wrote in Ephesians 5:33: "Nevertheless let each one of you in particular so love his own wife as himself, and let the wife see that she respect her husband." A marriage characterized by love and respect is pleasing in the sight of God.

## You've Got a Friend

Some people don't have a spouse or children, either by their own choice or from circumstances beyond their control. Jeremiah the prophet was commanded by God, "You shall not take a wife, nor shall you have sons or daughters in this place" (16:2). For many years, Jeremiah brought an unpopular message of repentance to a rebellious and disobedient people. After the destruction of Jerusalem, he began his book of Lamentations with these words, "How lonely sits the city that was full of people! How like a widow is she, who was great among the nations! ... All her friends have dealt treacherously with her; they have become her enemies" (1:1-2). Although Jeremiah was talking about Jerusalem, he may have felt the same sense of friendlessness as he was rejected and persecuted by his own people.

On one occasion, Jeremiah was put into a dungeon where he sank in the mire (Jeremiah 38:6). Alone and helpless, he might have died if not for the intervention of an unlikely ally named Ebed-Melech, an Ethiopian eunuch who was a servant of King Zedekiah. Ebed-Melech convinced the king to bring Jeremiah out of the dungeon. He not only brought ropes to pull Jeremiah out, but he also showed extra kindness by giving Jeremiah old clothes and rags to put under his armpits so that the ropes would not hurt him (v. 12). In Jeremiah's time of deepest need, God provided a friend to be a help and comfort to him. Later God commended Ebed-Melech and promised him deliverance from the destruction of Jerusalem because of his kindness to Jeremiah (39:16-18).

Another prophet, Elijah, found himself in need of a friend. Elijah told King Ahab that "there shall not be dew nor rain these years, except at my word" (1 Kings 17:1). God told Elijah to go to the Brook Cherith, where he could drink from the brook and be fed by ravens. After a while, God told Elijah to go to Zarephath where a widow would provide for him. God knew that Elijah needed more than food from the ravens. He also needed human interaction.

When Elijah asked the widow for some bread, she was at first reluctant to provide for him. She had only a little flour and oil to make bread for herself and her son. The widow was hesitant to give her son's only sustenance to a stranger, as any mother would be. Elijah assured her, "The bin of flour shall not be used up, nor shall the jar of oil run dry, until the day the LORD sends rain on the earth" (1 Kings 17:14). With great faith, the widow believed Elijah's promise, and "she and he and her household ate for many days" (v. 15).

As time passed, the widow's son got sick and died. Elijah prayed to God, and the child was brought back to life. Elijah then "gave him to his mother" (1 Kings 17:23). What a wonderful gift of life! God provided a friend to help Elijah during the lonely days of the famine, and Elijah in turn was able to help the widow by bringing her son back to life. Friends help one another during difficult times. As Solomon said, "A friend loves at all times, and a brother is born for adversity" (Proverbs 17:17).

Paul made many friends as he was traveling around the country starting churches wherever he went. At the end of many of his letters to churches and individuals, he greeted his friends by name. At the end of his second letter to Timothy, Paul wrote, "At my first defense no one stood with me, but all forsook me. May it not be charged against them. But the Lord stood with me and strengthened me" (2 Timothy 4:16-17). Paul discovered that he had some fair-weather friends who made themselves scarce when times got tough. Paul must have felt lonely and disappointed, but he knew that although everyone else forsook him, the Lord was with him. Rather than focusing on his discouragement, Paul was grateful for the friends who stayed with him. He told Timothy, "Only Luke is with me. Get Mark and bring him with you, for he is useful to me for ministry" (v. 11).

Jesus certainly knew the pain of loneliness. When Jesus started His ministry of preaching, teaching and healing, He was almost constantly surrounded by people. Multitudes followed Him expecting to see a miracle. With all those people around Him, Jesus hardly had time to be lonely. But despite His popularity, Jesus in His foreknowledge knew that He would be forsaken. After the Last Supper with His disciples, Jesus told them, "Indeed, the hour is coming, yes, has now come, that you will be scattered, each to his own, and will leave Me alone. And yet, I am not alone because my Father is with Me" (John 16:32).

As He prepared for the final agonizing moments of His life, knowing that He would be crucified, Jesus took His disciples to the Garden of Gethsemane. He chose His three closest friends – Peter, James and John – to accompany Him in the garden. Matthew wrote that Jesus began to feel sorrowful and deeply distressed. He made a simple request of His friends – to stay and watch with Him while He went to pray.

When Jesus came back, He found the disciples sleeping. In Matthew 26:40, Jesus said to Peter, "What! Could you not watch with Me one hour?" Peter had boldly declared that he would never deny Jesus and would die with Him if necessary. But during the time of Jesus' greatest need, Peter and the other disciples couldn't even keep their eyes open.

This happened not once, but three times. You can almost hear the disappointment and frustration in His voice as Jesus came back a third time and said to His disciples, "Are you still sleeping and resting? Behold, the hour is at hand, and the Son of Man is being betrayed into the hands of sinners" (Matthew 26:45). Imagine how lonely Jesus must have felt as He bore His heavy burden of sorrow all alone, forsaken by His best friends.

But the worst was still to come. As He hung on the cross, it seemed that even God had turned His back on His Son. In Matthew 27:46, Jesus cried out in anguish, "My God, My God, why have You forsaken Me?" Jesus understood the pain of loneliness, probably more than any of us could ever imagine.

Maybe you are feeling lonely right now. Perhaps you have been hurt or rejected by someone that you loved deeply, and you are finding it hard to reach out to others for fear of being hurt again. Jesus knows how you feel. The truth is you are not really alone at all.

## How to Be an Effective Friend

The best cure for loneliness is to find a friend. Here are a few guidelines for making and maintaining friendships.

• **Put Away Your Smartphone.** In this generation of smartphones, iPads, Facebook and Twitter, people are more connected than ever before but also more lonely. Many people have hundreds of Facebook friends but very few face-to-face friends. It is not unusual to see two people at a restaurant or other public place sitting next to each other, but both totally engrossed in their digital gadgets. They may be sending text messages, surfing the Internet or, ironically, playing an online game of "Words With Friends!" but they are not talking to each other.

If this is a familiar scenario between you and your friends or between you and your spouse, it may be time to make some changes. Plan a time in which you both decide to put away the cell phone, computer, television or whatever else is taking up your attention and just talk to each other face-to-face. Smile and look at each other in the eye. Tell each other about your day and just enjoy one another's company. Solomon was right when he said, "A man who has friends must himself be friendly" (Proverbs 18:24).

• **Be a Good Listener.** There are two kinds of people in the world – extroverts and introverts. Extroverts often talk too much while introverts don't talk enough. In his book *The Friendship Factor*, Alan Loy McGinnis told how he asked his popular friend to teach him how to talk to people. His friend told him that "the secret of being interesting is to be interested" (110). McGinnis also wrote, "You do not have to be witty and verbose to be a good conversationalist. You simply must know how to listen" (110). Sometimes you miss out on what a person is saying because you are thinking about what you are going to say next. The next time someone is talking to you, make a conscious effort to focus on that one person and really listen to what he or she is saying. Listen not only with your ears but also with your eyes and your facial expressions.

• **Be an Encourager.** McGinnis also suggested using the art of affirmation. Be liberal with praise. Don't try to flatter people, but look for things in a person you can sincerely compliment. Benjamin Franklin wrote, "Speak ill of no man, but speak all the good you know of everybody" (McGinnis, 50). Be an encourager, as the writer of Hebrews advised, "Let us consider one another in order to stir up love and good works" (Hebrews 10:24).

• **Cultivate Transparency.** Don't put on masks and try to be someone you are not. Be open and honest in your relationships. McGinnis said that many people are afraid to share too much of themselves for fear of rejection, but he explained that when people take off their masks, others are drawn to them. He wrote, "If we build more windows and fewer walls, we will have more friends."

• **Keep a Confidence Confident.** Don't be a gossip and tell everyone else what someone has shared with you in secret. Be a loyal friend. "He who covers a transgression seeks love, but he who repeats a matter separates friends" (Proverbs 17:9).

• **Don't Be Fooled by First Impressions.** When I graduated from college, I lived overseas for a few years, and I was always glad to get letters from friends back home. (This was in the days before email.) I got a letter in the mail from one of my college friends telling me about a guy at school who kept following her and wouldn't leave her alone. I wrote back to her, but I didn't hear from her for a few months. Finally, I wrote to her again and asked her if that guy was still following her around. It wasn't long before I got another letter from her. She wrote, "Yes, that guy *is* still following me around, and probably will for the next 50 years. We're engaged to be married!" Don't always dismiss people who seem annoying at first. You could miss out on a great friendship or a future spouse.

• **Look for Friends in the Right Places.** I got a flyer in the mail for a computer dating service that advertised, "Let us help you find your soulmate!" Many people are looking for a soulmate in the wrong places – in singles bars, night clubs, casinos, or through escort services, newspaper advertisements and, most frequently, on the Internet. Computers can be a wonderful tool for communication and information, but they can also be dangerous. If you like chatting with people online and hope to meet someone special, try to keep to safe sites, such as Churchof ChristSingles.com or other Christian singles websites.

Better yet, if you are lonely and need a friend, try to go where the people are. Join a bowling league, take an aerobics class, take a night class on some subject you have always enjoyed, or sign up for a team sport. Doing volunteer work is a great way to meet people. Take Meals on Wheels to shut-ins, be a mentor at a school and help a student learn to read, visit a nursing home and talk to some of the residents, work in a soup kitchen or homeless shelter. There are limitless opportunities for volunteer work. Your lonely days will soon become full when you spend time helping other people.

There's one other place you can go where you are sure to find a friend or two – church. Don't just be a pew warmer, sitting on the pew for an hour on Sunday and then rushing home after the service. Get involved in the work of the church. Go to the fellowship meals, attend the Bible classes and other special services. Invite people to your home for a fellowship activity. A Christian's best friends should be her friends at church, those who share her values and beliefs. Although you may be far away from home, when you spend time with other Christians you are with family.

## An All-Weather Friend

Maybe you have done all these things and you still feel friendless and alone. Or maybe you have a lot of acquaintances, but not one person who is a real soulmate, someone with whom you can share all your deepest thoughts, someone who will always be there for you.

In Psalm 139, David described his soulmate. He began, "O LORD, You have searched me and known me. You know my sitting down and my rising up; You understand my thought afar off. You comprehend my path and my lying down, and are acquainted with all my ways. For there is not a word on my tongue, but behold, O LORD, You know it altogether" (vv. 1-4).

Wouldn't it be great to have a friend who knows what you're going to say – even before you say it? God knows. Wouldn't it be great to have a friend who knows everything about you and still thinks you're wonderful? God does.

David continued in Psalm 139:7-10, "Where can I go from Your Spirit? Or where can I flee from Your presence? If I ascend into heaven, You are there. If I make my bed in hell, behold, You are there. If I take the wings of the morning, and dwell in the uttermost parts of the sea, even there Your hand shall lead me, and Your right hand shall hold me."

Wouldn't it be great to have a friend who is always there for you? God is. He'll be there when everything is coming up roses, or when you are going through the fire of affliction. God is not a *fair*-weather friend. He is an *all*-weather friend.

Jesus said to His apostles, "No longer do I call you servants, for a servant does not know what his master is doing; but I have called you friends, for all things I heard from My Father, I have made known to you" (John 15:15). Jesus also said just before He ascended into heaven, "Lo, I am with you always, even to the end of the age" (Matthew 28:20). This promise was not just for the apostles but also for us today. Jesus is always with you. If you are looking for a soulmate, try looking up. Jesus is the best friend you could ever have.

## Questions to Ponder

1. What was the one thing God saw of His creation that was not good (Genesis 2:18)?
2. How did Ebed-Melech show himself a friend to Jeremiah (Jeremiah 38:6-13)?
3. How did Elijah and the widow of Zarephath help one another (1 Kings 17:9-24)?
4. What did Paul reveal about some of his friends? Who strengthened him when everyone else forsook him (2 Timothy 4:11-17)?
5. In what ways did Jesus experience loneliness (Matthew 26:37-46; 27:46; John 16:32)?
6. Read Psalm 139:1-18. How do these verses show that God is the perfect soulmate?
7. What suggestions do you have for making and keeping friends?

# My True Friend

*How I long for a friend with a sympathizing ear,*
*Someone who will listen and really hear*
*All of my innermost thoughts and fears,*
*With a shoulder big enough to take all my tears.*
*Someone with an open heart and understanding eyes,*
*Who will hear me out and not criticize,*
*But just listen and try to understand,*
*And give me a hug and hold my hand.*
*But I do have a friend who really cares.*
*He sees all my tears and hears all my prayers.*
*He understands because He's been there too.*
*He knows all my hurts, and His love is true.*
*He knows all my faults and loves me just the same.*
*He is my true friend. Jesus is His name.*

# The Word on Loneliness

**Proverbs 17:17**

"A friend loves at all times, and a brother is born for adversity."

**Proverbs 18:24**

"A man who has friends must himself be friendly,
but there is a friend who sticks closer than a brother."

**Proverbs 27:17**

"As iron sharpens iron, so a man sharpens
the countenance of his friend."

**Ecclesiastes 4:9-10**

"Two are better than one because, they have a good reward for their labor. For if they fall, one will lift up his companion. But woe to him who is alone when he falls, for he has no one to help him up."

Chapter 2

# The Green-Eyed Monster

## *Jealousy*

William Shakespeare called it a "green-eyed monster." King Solomon said it was "as cruel as the grave" (Song of Solomon 8:6). They were both talking about jealousy. Someone has said, "If you are green with envy, you are ripe for trouble." Jealousy is often the cause of broken relationships, aggravated assault and even murder. Jealousy, or envy, if left unchecked, can lead to tragedy. One of the most extreme cases of jealousy is found in the sad story of Rachel and Leah.

### A Tale of Two Sisters

Sibling rivalry is quite common in most families. A little competition between brothers and sisters is healthy and normal. But when two sisters are married to the same man, that's just trouble with a capital T! Such was the case with Rachel and Leah.

It all started when Jacob fell in love with Rachel and asked for her hand in marriage. But Rachel's father tricked Jacob. After the wedding ceremony and the wedding night, Jacob woke the next day to find he was married to Leah, not his beloved Rachel. After protesting to his father-in-law, Jacob was soon allowed to marry Rachel also. And so began a struggle between the two sisters that would last for many years.

Leah knew that Jacob loved Rachel, but Leah was determined to win his love by producing children for him. She revealed the deep longings of her heart, even by the names that she chose for her children. We can read the birth announcements in Genesis 29:32-35. Leah named her first son Reuben, which means "see, a son." She even said, "The LORD has surely looked on my affliction. Now therefore, my husband will love me." Leah was giving a message to Jacob that said, "See? I gave you a son. Now will you love me as much as you love Rachel?"

Leah named her second son Simeon, which means "heard" because the Lord had heard that she was unloved (Genesis 29:33). Her third son was called Levi, which means "attached." Leah said, "Now this time my husband will become attached to me, because I have borne him three sons" (v. 34). Leah bore a fourth son and named him Judah, which means "praise." She declared, "Now I will praise the LORD" (v. 35).

Genesis 30:1-2 says that "Rachel envied her sister and said to Jacob, 'Give me children, or else I die!' And Jacob's anger was aroused against Rachel, and he said, 'Am I in the place of God, who has withheld from you the fruit of the womb?' " Do you see what jealousy does? It changes people. No longer was Rachel the sweet, beautiful young girl with whom Jacob had fallen in love. She had turned into an envious, angry, demanding woman, blaming her husband for her limitations. Jealousy not only changed Rachel but also the way Jacob felt toward her. Jealousy doesn't do anything to help a relationship. It just drives people further apart.

Rachel then gave her handmaiden, Bilhah, to Jacob with the hope that she could have a child through her. Bilhah gave birth to a son, whom Rachel named Dan, which means "judge" because God had judged Rachel's case. Bilhah bore a second son, whose name was very revealing of Rachel's true motives. He was named Naphtali, which means "wrestling." Genesis 30:8 records these words that Rachel said: "With great wrestlings I have wrestled with my sister, and indeed I have prevailed." Now we know the real reason why Rachel wanted children. It was not just the maternal instinct kicking in. It was so she could prevail over her sister. Rachel wanted to be the best, the most loved and the most popular. Jealousy made her a very selfish person.

Leah's attitude was just as bad as Rachel's. She gave her handmaid, Zilpah to Jacob as a means to acquire more sons. Leah named Zilpah's son Gad, which means "troop." Leah was sending a message to Rachel that said, "I have a whole troop of sons, and you don't have any."

Genesis 30:14-16 reveals another episode in the saga of Rachel and Leah. Rachel asked Leah for some of her son's mandrakes. Leah said, "Is it a small matter that you have taken away my husband? Would you take away my son's mandrakes also?" A mandrake was a plant that was often used in ancient times as a means of promoting conception in barren women. In desperation, Rachel made a deal with Leah. "He will lie with you tonight for your son's mandrakes." Poor unsuspecting Jacob. When he came home that evening, he had a surprise waiting for him. Leah demanded, "You must come in to me, for I have surely hired you with my son's mandrakes."

For Leah, this struggle was no longer a test to see who could win the love of Jacob. It was a battle to see who could produce the most children because more children meant more power and prestige. Jacob was no longer the respected and revered husband. He had been reduced to a male prostitute, an object by which Leah could gain what she wanted. Jealousy turned the poor, unloved, desperate Leah into a manipulative shrew.

After many years of suffering the stigma of infertility, Rachel finally did bear Jacob a son, whom she named Joseph, meaning "Jehovah will increase." Years later, she travailed in hard labor one last time. She brought another son into the world, but tragically lost her own life. In her dying breath, she named him Ben-Oni (son of my sorrow), but Jacob called him Benjamin.

Rachel had said earlier, "I have wrestled with my sister, and indeed I have prevailed." But did she really prevail? Was all the wrestling really worth it? Who really won this struggle between the two sisters? The truth is nobody won. All the years of struggle had produced a family of 12 sons, who shared the same attitudes as Rachel and Leah. The spirit of jealousy was passed onto the next generation as we will see from the story of Joseph and his older brothers.

## The Next Generation

Because he was the first son of Rachel, Joseph was Jacob's favorite, and Jacob made no bones about it. He gave Joseph a special coat of many colors, which made Joseph's older brothers green with envy. These brothers took their jealousy to a whole new level – a much more evil and sinister level. Their jealousy toward Joseph became so intense that they wanted to kill their own brother.

Genesis 37 tells the story of how the 10 older brothers got their chance to get rid of the source of their anger. First, they threw Joseph into a pit and intended to leave him there to die. Then Judah had the idea to sell Joseph as a slave. Only 17 years old, the young Joseph had to travel alone to Egypt, all because of the jealousy of his brothers.

More than 20 years passed before Joseph saw his brothers again. During that time, Joseph had been promoted to the second in command under Pharaoh in Egypt. A famine had ravaged the land, and Joseph's job was to sell grain to anyone who needed it. One day, who should come looking for grain but Joseph's own brothers? They did not recognize their long lost brother, but Joseph recognized them.

At first, Joseph treated his brothers roughly and harshly. He wasn't trying to be mean or vindictive. He was just testing them to see if they had changed. Joseph may have spent many nights worrying and wondering about his little brother, Benjamin. Now that Joseph was gone, Benjamin would become the favorite son. Joseph may have wondered if his brothers were treating Benjamin in the same way they had treated him.

The final test came for Joseph's brothers when Joseph told them to leave Benjamin with him to be his slave, and the rest of them could go free. Judah, the same one who had suggested selling Joseph as a slave so many years ago now bowed before Joseph and pleaded for the life of Benjamin. In Genesis 44:18-34, Judah gave a touching speech about how his father would be grieved if Benjamin were taken from him. Judah asked that he be taken as a slave instead so that Benjamin could be free to go back to his father. That was exactly what Joseph wanted to hear. He could contain himself no longer as he tearfully revealed his true identity.

Joseph could see that his brothers had changed over the years. No longer were they thinking of themselves, but they were more concerned about their father and his happiness. The spirit of jealousy was gone. The curse of jealousy had stricken this family for years, not only from Rachel and Leah but also from Jacob and Esau, Isaac and Ishmael, Sarah and Hagar. With Joseph's love and forgiveness, the curse of jealousy was broken. Joseph invited his father and all his brothers and their families to come to Egypt to live. Finally they could be one big happy family.

## How to Root Out Jealousy

Everybody gets jealous sometimes. You've probably felt a tinge of jealousy when your brother or sister got more attention than you, or when your co-worker got the promotion you wanted, or you noticed an attractive person amorously eyeing your spouse or loved one, or your friend got the car that you wanted. Feeling a little jealous is normal, but allowing jealousy to escalate can be dangerous.

Jealousy is like a little plant that grows rapidly. It starts small but when nourished, it sprouts into anger, bitterness and rage. Jealousy must be rooted out while it is small, before it completely ruins your relationships and your reputation. So, how do you get rid of those niggling feelings of jealousy? Here are a few suggestions.

• **Have an Attitude of Gratitude**. Jealous feelings start when you see something that someone else has and you want it for yourself. So what if your neighbor has a brand new Lexus and you have an old Chevette? Be grateful that you have a car. Remember the old adage: "I complained because I had no shoes until I met a man who had no feet." When you start to feel jealous of someone else's possessions, success or relationships, take time to count your blessings. Take Paul's advice in 1 Thessalonians 5:18, "In everything give thanks; for this is the will of God in Christ Jesus for you."

• **Don't Compare Yourself With Others**. That was the mistake both Rachel and Leah made. Rachel envied Leah because she was able to bear children while Leah envied Rachel because she was Jacob's favorite. They both wanted what the other had, and they were both miserable.

When you compare yourself to someone else who is more successful, more popular or more talented than you, that makes you feel like a lesser person. You may even get angry at the other person for making you recognize your shortcomings. Don't blame others for your shortcomings. Maybe you need to work a little harder to achieve success or work on developing your talents to a greater degree. Do what you can to improve yourself. Envying other people's achievements doesn't help you at all. It only makes you feel worse. Paul said in 2 Corinthians 10:12, "For we dare not class ourselves or compare ourselves with those who commend themselves. But they, measuring themselves by themselves, and comparing themselves among themselves, are not wise."

• **Develop a Sense of Trust**. Have you ever had a friend who became angry with you because you were spending too much time with another friend? Or maybe you've heard someone yell, "Stay away from my girl!" or "Stay away from my boyfriend." A person who acts that way sees people as possessions, not people. A person who is extremely jealous is insecure in his or her relationships. Jealousy often results in a suspicious mind with eyes that see betrayal, even when it does not exist.

A perfect example of the tragic results of jealousy is found in Shakespeare's *Othello*. In this story, Othello was convinced that his lovely wife, Desdemona, was having an affair with Cassio even though there was no evidence to prove that accusation. Othello became so obsessed with the idea that his wife was being unfaithful to him that he ended up killing both Cassio and Desdemona. When he finally learned that Desdemona had been faithful to him all along, Othello felt so guilt-ridden that he killed himself as well.

Jealousy can destroy loving relationships. First Corinthians 13:4 says that "love does not envy." If you truly love someone, you will trust that person. If you suspect that a loved one is having an improper relationship with someone else, by all means talk to him about it. Don't always jump to conclusions. A loving relationship is built on a foundation of trust and respect.

• **Recognize That Jealousy Is From the Devil**. Paul mentioned the works of the flesh in Galatians 5:19-21. Among this list of sins, such as murder, adultery and drunkenness, you will also find jealousies and envy. Satan wants you to be jealous of others because once you give in to feelings of jealousy, you give in to sin. James 3:15-16 says, "This wisdom does not descend from above, but is earthly, sensual, demonic. For where envy and self-seeking exist, confusion and every evil thing are there." Don't let Satan have his way. Destroy those jealous thoughts before they destroy you. Don't be jealous; be zealous. Especially be zealous in reading the Word of God and doing the will of God.

## Questions to Ponder

1. Read Genesis 30:1-2. Why did Rachel envy her sister? What did her envy cause her to do? How did Jacob's feelings toward Rachel change because of her envy?
2. Read Genesis 37:3-4. Why did Joseph's brothers hate him? Do you think the brothers learned this attitude from their mothers?
3. Read Genesis 50:15-21. How did Joseph finally break the cycle of jealousy in the family?
4. What are some things that make you feel jealous? What can you do to overcome these feelings of jealousy?
5. How can an attitude of gratitude help to overcome jealousy?
6. Is jealousy a sin (Galatians 5:19-21)? Why or why not?
7. How can we develop a greater sense of trust so that we do not become jealous of others?

# Jealousy

*Jealousy is as cruel as the grave,*
*Enticing you to become its slave,*
*Angry to see someone else's gain,*
*Looking at others with bitter disdain.*
*Only a seed, but when allowed to grow,*
*Unrevealed attitudes start to show.*
*Suspicious thoughts soon lead to anger and wrath.*
*You'll be sorry you walked down Jealousy's path.*

# The Word on Jealousy

**Proverbs 14:30**

"A sound heart is life to the body,
but envy is rottenness to the bones."

**Song of Solomon 8:6**

"For love is as strong as death, jealousy as cruel as the grave.
Its flames are flames of fire, a most vehement flame."

**1 Corinthians 13:4**

"Love suffers long and is kind, love does not envy."

**James 3:16**

"For where envy and self-seeking exist, confusion
and every evil thing are there."

Chapter 3

# Plagued With Fears

## *Fear*

Imagine that you are driving down the road in your car. Suddenly, from out of nowhere, you see a big truck coming straight toward you in your lane. Your heart starts beating wildly, your stomach feels queasy, and you suddenly ache all over. Is there something wrong with you? No, you are experiencing fear, a normal reaction to a dangerous circumstance.

Now imagine that you have these same symptoms every day, even in non-threatening situations. It seems that your life is plagued with fears. You are not alone. About 19 million Americans feel the same way.

According to the National Institute of Mental Heath, 5.3 million Americans, ages 18 to 54, have some type of specific phobia. But fear is nothing new. In fact, it is as old as Adam.

### Hide and Seek

When God made Adam and Eve, He put them in a beautiful garden paradise where they had everything they could ever want or need. But one day, everything changed. Genesis 3:9-10 says, "Then the LORD God called to Adam and said to him, 'Where are you?' So he said, 'I heard Your voice in the garden, and I was afraid because I was naked; and I hid myself.' "

Adam was afraid of God because he knew he had sinned by disobeying

God's one command to refrain from eating the fruit from the tree of knowledge of good and evil. Fear was the direct result of sin. Eating a forbidden fruit may not seem like such a big thing, but any disobedience of God's command is sin. For the first time, Adam and Eve trembled and quivered as they were gripped by the icy cold hand of fear. They tried to hide from God, but it was futile. God is an expert at hide and seek. He always knows just where to find us.

## Saul and David

The Bible tells of another person who hid in fear although he was supposed to be a fearless leader. God told Samuel to anoint Saul as the first king of Israel. First Samuel 10:21-22 says that when Samuel revealed Saul as the chosen king, the people couldn't find him. The Lord Himself said, "There he is, hidden among the equipment." When they pulled him out, they found Saul was "taller than any of the people from his shoulders up" (v. 23). Saul certainly looked the part. On the outside, he was tall, strong and regal, but on the inside, Saul was full of fear and anxiety. In spite of his reluctance, God helped Saul to become a popular king.

Unfortunately, Saul began to do things his way instead of God's way. He disobeyed a direct command of God. In 1 Samuel 15:24, Saul explained to Samuel his reason for disobeying God. "I have transgressed the commandment of the LORD and your words, because I feared the people and obeyed their voice." Saul's fear led him to make wrong decisions. Samuel then uttered the words that Saul feared the most. "The LORD has rejected you from being king over Israel" (v. 26).

First Samuel 17 tells of Goliath, a giant soldier in the Philistine army who challenged the army of Israel to fight against him. Verse 11 says, "When Saul and all Israel heard these words of the Philistines, they were dismayed and greatly afraid." As king, Saul should have been a courageous leader; instead he cowered in fear, and his whole army followed his example.

You probably know the rest of the story. David, the shepherd boy accepted Goliath's challenge and killed him with a sling and a small stone. He became a hero in the eyes of the Israelite people and was invited to live at Saul's house. According to 1 Samuel 18:12, "Saul was afraid of

David, because the LORD was with him, but had departed from Saul." Why was Saul, the mighty king, afraid of David, the lowly shepherd? Verses 14-15 continue to explain: "And David behaved wisely in all his ways, and the LORD was with him. Therefore, when Saul saw that he behaved very wisely, he was afraid of him."

People are afraid of things or individuals who make them feel threatened. Saul was threatened by David's popularity and favor with God. Saul knew he had been rejected by God because of his disobedience, but rather than repent and turn to God, he chose to blame David for his demise. His fear of failure and rejection began a dangerous downward spiral.

Saul tried to have David killed. Saul pursued David in the wilderness for years to no avail. In the meantime, Saul still struggled with his ongoing war with the Philistines. First Samuel 28:5 says, "When Saul saw the army of the Philistines, he was afraid, and his heart trembled greatly." In his desperation to find out the outcome of the war, Saul disguised himself and consulted a medium, even though he had cut off all mediums and spiritists from the land. He broke his own rule and asked the medium to conduct a séance and bring the prophet Samuel up from the dead. The medium did not have the power to bring up Samuel, but God did. God allowed Samuel to give this chilling prophecy to Saul: "Tomorrow you and your sons will be with me. The LORD will also deliver the army of Israel into the hand of the Philistines" (v. 19).

The next verse shows Saul's reaction to the news. "Immediately Saul fell full length on the ground, and was dreadfully afraid because of the words of Samuel. And there was no strength in him, for he had eaten no food all day or all night" (1 Samuel 28:20). Saul was quite literally paralyzed by fear. He was sapped of his strength and even his sanity. The once mighty king was now a pathetic, trembling soul. Samuel's prophecy came true the very next day. Saul was wounded in a battle against the Philistines. He asked his armor bearer to thrust him through with the sword because he was afraid the Philistines would torture and abuse him. Because the armor bearer would not kill Saul, Saul killed himself (31:3-4). What a tragic end to the life of a king who had such great potential.

David became king after Saul. He was the most beloved and well-known king in all of Israel's history. What made David so different from Saul? Why was David not afraid of the giant Goliath? If we go back to 1 Samuel 17:47, we can see that David's faith in God overcame his fear of the enemy. He declared, "Then all this assembly shall know that the LORD does not save with sword and spear; for the battle is the LORD's, and He will give you into our hands." With that kind of faith and confidence, how could David lose?

His battle with Goliath was easy compared to his continuing battle with King Saul. David was a fugitive, living in the wilderness and hiding in caves to escape the wrath of Saul. Many of David's best psalms were written while he was on the run. Sometimes David was afraid. He admitted in Psalm 56:3, "Whenever I am afraid, I will trust in You."

In Psalm 27, David wrote, "The LORD is my light and my salvation. Whom shall I fear? The LORD is the strength of my life; of whom shall I be afraid?" (v. 1). David had every reason to be afraid, but he took all his fears and anxieties to the Lord in prayer. God answered his prayers and caused David to prosper.

Do you sometimes feel paralyzed by fear? Do you have phobias and anxieties that hold you back from doing all the things you want to do? What you need is a "David attitude" instead of a "Saul complex." Saul succumbed to his fears, but David was able to overcome his fears through his faith in God.

## How to Dispel Fear

Let's face it. We all have fears. Some of the most common fears are fear of flying, heights, public speaking, spiders, and closed or open spaces. What is the best way to deal with these fears?

• **Face It.** Psychologists say the best way to overcome fear is to face it. If you are afraid of flying, the most common reaction is to avoid flying at all times. The best thing to do is to get on that plane and fly to your destination. It may be daunting at first, but the more often you fly, the more you will realize that flying is not so frightening after all. You may even start to enjoy flying and look forward to that next long trip.

You may be able to conquer your fear with the use of a technique called "virtual therapy exposure" which is often used in anxiety disorder clinics. With the help of virtual reality computer graphics, you can visualize the object of your fear. The 3-D picture of a spider, a cat, the inside of an airplane or elevator, or even an audience listening to your speech is a safe way to face fear in a non-threatening setting.

• **Feel the Emotion**. Another way to deal with fears is suggested in the best-selling book *Tuesdays With Morrie*. Mitch Albom wrote this touching tribute to his friend and mentor, Morrie Schwartz, who was suffering from amyotrophic lateral sclerosis (ALS) or Lou Gehrig's Disease. Though Morrie's body was slowly disintegrating, his enthusiasm and love of life never wavered.

Morrie gave Mitch some excellent advice on facing fears. He suggested that instead of trying to avoid fear or any other painful emotion, you should immerse yourself in it. Allow yourself to feel the emotion, and then detach from it. Say to yourself, "Okay, this is fear," and then step away from it.

"If you let the fear inside, if you pull it on like a familiar shirt, then you can say to yourself, 'All right, it's just fear. I don't have to let it control me. I see it for what it is'" (104-05).

• **Renounce It**. Another approach to fear is expressed by Neil T. Anderson in his book, *The Bondage Breaker*. Anderson believes that fear is a tool of the devil to weaken your faith. He suggests that you write a list of your fears, and then renounce them. If you are afraid of death, say *out loud* in a forceful voice, "I renounce my fear of death, because God has not given me a spirit of fear" (216-17). Do the same thing with all the other fears on your list. By renouncing your fears, you are strengthening your faith. Paul said in 2 Timothy 1:7, "For God has not given us a spirit of fear, but of power and of love and of a sound mind." God does not give us fears. He gives us the power to overcome them.

• **Pray About Your Fears**. Have you ever been so afraid that your knees knocked together? The book of Daniel tells the story of Belshazzar, the king of Babylon, who saw a hand writing on the wall. Daniel 5:6 says, "Then the king's countenance changed, and his thoughts troubled him, so that the joints of his hips were loosened and his knees knocked against each other." That reminds me of a saying that I once read, "When your knees knock, kneel on them." The best cure for fear is prayer. David knew the power of prayer. He wrote in Psalm 34:4, "I sought the LORD, and He heard me, and delivered me from all my fears." David often poured out his heart to God, and through prayer he found comfort, strength and courage.

• **Shift Your Focus**. Sometimes overcoming fear is as simple as shifting your focus. If you keep your mind focused on positive thoughts, rather than on the source of your fear, then you won't be overcome by fear. An example of this is found in the New Testament. Matthew 14 tells how the apostles were in a boat late at night when they saw a ghostly figure walking on the water. They were afraid until they realized that it was Jesus. Then Peter asked if he could walk on the water too, and Jesus said, "Come" (vv. 28-29).

"But when he saw that the wind was boisterous, he was afraid; and beginning to sink he cried out, saying, 'Lord, save me!'" (Matthew 14:30) As long as Peter kept his mind and his eyes focused on Jesus he was able to walk on the water. But once he started to look at the winds and the waves, he took his focus off Jesus and began to be afraid. When you look around and see violence, terrorism and war all around you, it is easy to become afraid. But you need to keep your mind focused on Jesus, "looking unto Jesus, the author and finisher of our faith" (Hebrews 12:2).

Martin Luther King Jr. made this observation: "Fear knocked at the door. Faith answered. There was no one there." That just means that when fear comes, let faith answer the door, and fear will go away. Isaiah summed it up best: "Behold, God is my salvation, I will trust and not be afraid; for YAH, the LORD is my strength and song; He also has become my salvation" (12:2).

## Questions to Ponder

1. Why was Adam afraid (Genesis 3:8-11)?
2. Why was Saul afraid of David (1 Samuel 18:12)?
3. Why was David not afraid of Goliath (1 Samuel 17:45-47)?
4. Was David ever afraid? How did he overcome his fears (Psalm 34:4; 56:3-4)?
5. What do you think of Morrie Schwartz's suggestion to feel the emotion of fear, immerse yourself in it, and then detach from it?

6. What do you think of Neil T. Anderson's idea to renounce your fears out loud?

7. What are some of your fears? What do you do to overcome them?

# A Sonnet to Fear

*Fear is a friend that protects me from harm.*
*It warns me when something does not seem right.*
*Fear – that adrenaline shot in the arm –*
*Is my stimulus to flee or to fight.*
*But fear can easily become my foe*
*When I am plagued by unrealistic fears*
*That follow me, no matter where I go,*
*Reducing me to shivers, dread and tears.*
*Lord, please be with me when I am afraid,*
*And help me to bear my anxiety*
*With courage and faith that will never fade.*
*I know you will always be there with me.*
*Lord, help me be like David when he prayed,*
*"I will trust in You when I am afraid."*

# The Word on Fear

**Psalm 27:1**

"The LORD is my light and my salvation. Whom shall I fear? The LORD is the strength of my life; of whom shall I be afraid?"

**Psalm 34:4**

"I sought the LORD, and He heard me, and delivered me from all my fears."

**Isaiah 41:10**

"Fear not, for I am with you; be not dismayed, for I am your God. I will strengthen you, yes, I will help you, I will uphold you with My righteous right hand."

**2 Timothy 1:7**

"For God has not given us a spirit of fear, but of power and of love and of a sound mind."

Chapter 4

# The Grasshopper Syndrome

## *Low Self-Esteem*

Picture yourself in an elementary school classroom, right after the teacher has asked a question. You would probably see several hands waving in the air and hear the voices of children saying, "Oh! Oh! I know." They are enthusiastically vying for the teacher's attention as they strive to be first to answer the question correctly. You would probably see at least one other child sitting at the back of the class with his head down, hoping that the teacher doesn't call on him. He is afraid of being ridiculed if he answers the question wrong. Even if he knows the answer, he doesn't want to volunteer the information in case people think he is a know-it-all. It is much easier to sit in silent sadness, allowing others to get all the attention. That child is showing signs of low self-esteem.

People with low self-esteem have a very low opinion of themselves. They typically think and say things like:

- "I'm not good at anything."
- "Nobody likes me."
- "I don't fit in."
- "There's something wrong with me."

People with low self-esteem compare themselves with others and feel they don't measure up. They suffer from the "grasshopper syndrome."

## Grasshoppers and Dead Dogs

After Moses led the Israelites out of Egypt, God commanded him to send 12 men to spy out the land of Canaan, which was to be their new home. The 12 men inspected the land for 40 days, and then came back to give their reports. Two of the spies, Joshua and Caleb, told the people that it was a land flowing with milk and honey and that God would help them to claim what was theirs.

The 10 other spies brought a different report. They saw the fertile land and the luscious fruit of the fields, but they were more concerned about the giants who inhabited the land. "We are not able to go up against the people, for they are stronger than we," they complained. "There we saw the giants … and we were like grasshoppers in our own sight, and so we were in their sight" (Numbers 13:31, 33). Although Joshua and Caleb saw themselves as conquerors who could overtake the enemy and take the land with God's help, the remaining 10 spies saw themselves as grasshoppers, weak and inferior to the mighty giants.

An even more extreme example of low self-esteem is found in 2 Samuel 9:3-8. David had become king after Saul died. David learned that Mephibosheth, the son of David's best friend, Jonathan, was still alive. David asked one of his servants to bring Mephibosheth to meet him. Bowing down before the king, Mephibosheth said, "What is your servant, that you should look upon such a dead dog as I?" (v. 8). Mephibosheth's opinion of himself was the lowest of the low. He didn't just think of himself as a dog. He thought of himself as a dead dog – totally useless and insignificant. What a great encouragement it must have been to Mephibosheth when David invited him to eat bread at the king's table and be treated as one of the king's sons.

## Excuses, Excuses

Even great leaders and people who seem to be full of confidence can suffer from low self-esteem. One of the greatest leaders of all time was Moses. He boldly stood before Pharaoh and demanded, "Let my people go!" Later, he led God's people out of Egypt and into the wilderness for 40 years where he taught them God's commandments and prepared them to enter the Promised Land. But when Moses was first called by God, he was a very reluctant prophet. A close reading of Exodus 3 reveals that he was full of excuses. God spoke to Moses from a burning bush in the desert and told him to "bring My people, the children of Israel, out of Egypt."

"But Moses said to God, 'Who am I that I should go to Pharaoh, and that I should bring the children of Israel out of Egypt?' " (Exodus 3:10-11). In other words, he showed a lack of *confidence*. He felt unable to do the task that God asked of him. This is a common trait of people with low self-esteem. They think, "I can't," instead of thinking, "I can." They don't seem to realize that success comes in "cans," not "can'ts."

God assured Moses that He would be with him, but Moses was still unconvinced. He asked, "When I come to the children of Israel and say to them, 'The God of your fathers has sent me to you,' and they say to me, 'What is his name?' what shall I say to them?" (Exodus 3:13). This is another common trait of people with low self-esteem. They think, "I don't know what to say." Fear of rejection or ridicule can make silence a much safer option. Moses not only felt a lack of confidence, but also a lack of *competence*. He didn't feel he was up to the challenge.

God again told Moses that he would be with him and would give him the tools he would need to succeed. But Moses was ready with another excuse. In Exodus 4:1, he said, "But suppose they will not believe me or listen to my voice; suppose they say 'The LORD has not appeared to you.' " Moses had a lack of *conviction*. He believed in God, but he didn't believe in himself or in his ability to deliver the message adequately and boldly. Many people feel that way today. They are plagued with thoughts such as, "Nobody listens to me, nobody cares what I think, so why should I even try to say anything?"

God patiently answered Moses' doubts by showing him the miracles he could do with God's help, such as turning a rod into a snake. Moses responded with yet another excuse. He said he wasn't eloquent but was slow of speech and slow of tongue. Finally he pleaded in Exodus 4:13, "O my Lord, please send by the hand of whomever else You may send." Moses had a lack of *courage*. Even though God had continually encouraged Moses and showed His power and presence, Moses was afraid to do what God asked. Instead of saying, "Here I am, send me," Moses was saying, "Please send somebody else."

You would think that after all these excuses, God would have given up on Moses, but God never gives up. He believed in Moses' ability to do the task, even when Moses didn't believe in himself. God even gave Moses a helper, so he wouldn't have to go alone. Moses' brother, Aaron, went along to be his spokesman. In spite of his lack of confidence, competence, conviction and courage, Moses became a wise, bold and fearless leader for the people of Israel with God's help. If God can do that for Moses, He can do it for you too.

## His Image

Low self-esteem often stems from childhood experiences. Some people didn't get enough attention or affection as children. A child whose parents were perfectionists may have felt she could never measure up to their expectations. Other causes of low self-esteem are sibling rivalry, frequent criticism, childhood abuse or past failures.

Josh McDowell wrote an excellent book on self-esteem called *His Image, My Image*. He defined a good self-image as "seeing yourself as God sees you – no more and no less" (35). In his book, McDowell listed three basic needs that every person has. They are:

1. The need to feel loved, or a sense of belonging.
2. The need to feel acceptable, or a sense of worthiness.
3. The need to feel adequate, or a sense of competence.

McDowell went on to suggest that we should think of self-esteem as "resting on a three-legged stool." The seat of the stool is a person's self-image while the three legs of the stool are the basic needs – belonging, worthiness and competence. If any one of these three legs is damaged, the person's entire self image is unstable and shaky. Thankfully, there is someone who can meet all these needs (100).

### A Sense of Belonging

The love of God is made manifest throughout the Old and New Testaments. In Jeremiah 31:3, God said, "I have loved you with an everlasting love."

One of the most quoted verses in the New Testament, John 3:16 tells of God's love – "For God so loved the world that He gave His only begotten Son, that whosoever believes in Him should not perish but have everlasting life."

First John 3:1 says, "Behold, what manner of love the Father has bestowed on us, that we should be called children of God!" We have a sense of belonging because we belong to God who loved us so much that He sent His Son to die for us.

### A Sense of Worthiness

Genesis 1:27 tells us, "So God created man in His own image; in the image of God He created him; male and female He created them." David wrote in Psalm 139:14, "I will praise You, for I am fearfully and wonderfully made." Although evolutionists try to tell us that we were made not much higher than the animals, God tells us in Psalm 8:5 that we were made "a little lower than the angels."

God wants us to know that we are special. "But you are a chosen generation, a royal priesthood, a holy nation, His own special people" (1 Peter 2:9). We have a sense of worthiness because we were made in God's image. As one little boy aptly declared, "God made me, and God don't make no junk!"

### A Sense of Competence

We have already seen how Moses made excuses when God called him to go to Egypt. He felt incapable of doing what God asked him to do. While Moses was saying, "I can't," God was proclaiming, "I AM!" (Exodus 3:14). Paul said in Philippians 4:13, "I can do all things through Christ who strengthens me." We have a sense of competence because of Jesus.

## How to Raise Low Self-Esteem

• **Use Positive Words**. Every morning when you get up, look at yourself in the mirror and say, "I am made in the image of God. I am fearfully and wonderfully made. I can do all things through Christ who strengthens me." Say it like you mean it! Throughout the day, whenever you feel inadequate, say or think these same words to yourself over and over until they become part of your thought pattern. Putting up Post-its with encouraging verses or words around your mirror at home or your computer at work are also sure ways to ingrain these sayings in your mind.

• **Dwell on Your Strengths, Not Your Weaknesses**. In the book of Judges, an angel appeared to Gideon and said, "The LORD is with you, you mighty man of valor." Gideon replied that he was "the least in [his] father's house" (Judges 6:12, 15). Gideon was dwelling on his insignificance while the angel saw his potential. Don't think about all the things you can't do or don't do well. Concentrate on what you can do. Solomon wrote, "Whatever your hand finds to do, do it with your might" (Ecclesiastes 9:10).

• **Use Your Talents**. In Jesus' parable of the talents, the one-talent man was afraid and hid his talent in the ground (Matthew 25:25). He was punished for not using what had been given to him by his master. Don't bury your talents in the ground. Use them to help others. If you like working with children, offer to baby-sit for a young couple or help with the youth group at church. If you like to cook or bake, make a meal for a family or individual in need. If you are good with a hammer, volunteer to work with Habitat for Humanity. Using your talents to help others will be a great benefit to yourself as well.

• **Learn From the Past**. Do some self-analysis to discover why you have low self-esteem. It might be necessary to talk to a counselor about unresolved issues from your childhood. Don't let the past determine your future. Learn from past mistakes, but live in the present.

• **Don't Let Others Drag You Down**. You may feel inferior because of other people's criticism and unrealistic expectations. Listen to criticism and try to learn from it, but don't let others drag you down. Eleanor Roosevelt was quoted as saying, "No one can make you feel inferior without your consent."

God can help you overcome feelings of low self-esteem. Just as a lowly caterpillar changes to a beautiful butterfly by a process called metamorphosis, so you can also be transformed. As Paul said in Romans 12:2, "And do not be conformed to this world, but be transformed by the renewing of your mind." You can renew your mind by changing the way you think about yourself. Try to see yourself as God sees you – no more and no less. Remember that God loves you, He made you in His image, and you can do all things through Christ who strengthens you.

## Questions to Ponder

1. What are some causes of low self-esteem?
2. How did Mephibosheth feel about himself (2 Samuel 9:8)?
3. In Exodus chapters 3 and 4, how did Moses show a lack of confidence, competence, conviction and courage?
4. What does it mean that "God created man in His own image" (Genesis 1:27)?
5. What are the three basic needs according to Josh McDowell?
6. What are some ways you can "renew your mind" and think differently about yourself?
7. According to 1 Peter 2:9, what makes you special?

# Metamorphosis

*I was a caterpillar in a dark cocoon*
*Until you came and took me from that lonely room.*
*You were a butterfly; you taught me how to fly*
*To a land of happiness and lullabies.*
*I was a burnt out star against the ebon night*
*Until I shone as a reflection of your light.*
*You were the moon; you taught me how to shine,*
*Until the light reflected through me was mine.*
*I was a caged songbird who couldn't even sing.*
*I sat in silence, staring through a metal ring.*
*You were the locksmith. You held the key.*
*You touched the lock, unlatched the door, and set me free.*
*You've been a friend to me, so faithful and so true.*
*Through all the years, I've learned so much from watching you.*
*You taught me very well. You set me free.*
*Now I can fly and I can shine. I hold the key.*

# The Word on Low Self-Esteem

**Psalm 8:4-5**

"What is man that You are mindful of him, and the son of man that You visit him? For You have made him a little lower than the angels, and You have crowned him with glory and honor."

**Psalm 139:14**

"I will praise You, for I am fearfully and wonderfully made."

**Romans 8:37**

"Yet in all these things we are more than conquerors through Him who loved us."

**Philippians 4:13**

"I can do all things through Christ who strengthens me."

Chapter 5

# An Unpopular Subject

## *Sin*

I once heard a speaker describing former President Calvin Coolidge as a man of few words. To illustrate the fact, he told of a certain Sunday morning when President Coolidge went to church by himself because his wife was ill and couldn't attend. When he returned from church, his wife asked how the service went. "Good," he replied. Wanting to know more details, Mrs. Coolidge asked what the sermon was about. Mr. Coolidge answered, "Sin." Exasperated, his wife asked, "Well, what did the preacher say about sin?" President Coolidge thought a moment and then said, "He was against it."

Many preachers today would rather speak about grace, love or prosperity than to speak against sin because it has become an unpopular subject. In our modern culture, sin has been redefined. Years ago, an unmarried man and woman who were living together unmarried were said to be "living in sin." Now the practice of living together is commonly accepted. Abortion is no longer regarded as the murder of an unborn child but a woman's "right to choose." A homosexual couple is not "committing what is shameful," as described in Romans 1:27, but they are showing "gay pride." No matter what our society calls it, in God's eyes, sin is still sin.

### Eve Deceived

The originator of sin was Satan, "that serpent of old, called the

Devil and Satan, who deceives the whole world" (Revelation 12:9). Eve committed the first sin because she was deceived (2 Corinthians 11:3). Genesis 3 tells how that crafty serpent was able to convince Eve to eat of the fruit of the tree of the knowledge of good and evil. First, he asked her, "Has God indeed said, 'You shall not eat of every tree of the garden?' " (Genesis 3:1). Satan tried to confuse Eve and cause her to doubt God's command.

Second, he said, "You shall not surely die" (Genesis 3:4). Satan lied to Eve to make her think she could do whatever she wanted and there would be no consequences for her action. Third, he said, "In the day you eat of it your eyes will be opened, and you will be like God, knowing good and evil" (v. 5). Satan went further by convincing Eve that not only would nothing bad happen to her if she ate the fruit, but that it would actually be good for her. Then Eve took of the forbidden fruit and also gave some to Adam. Immediately after they disobeyed God's command, Adam and Eve felt something they had never experienced before – shame and embarrassment. From that moment on, their whole world was changed because of sin.

## David's Dark Side

We saw in a previous chapter how David's great faith and trust in God sustained him during difficult circumstances. In both 1 Samuel 13:14 and Acts 13:22, he is described as "a man after God's own heart." But even David had a dark side.

In 2 Samuel 11, King David lusted after the bathing beauty, Bathsheba, despite the fact she was married to Uriah the Hittite, one of the soldiers in David's army. David's one-night stand with Bathsheba led to an unwanted pregnancy. David's first response was to lure Uriah from the battlefield and into his wife's bedroom to give the impression that Uriah was the father of the child. When Uriah's loyalty to the king's army prevented him from doing this, David arranged to have him killed in battle. This time his plan succeeded. Within a year, David was at home with his new wife Bathsheba and their beloved baby boy. He had emerged from his predicament unscathed – or so it seemed.

In 2 Samuel 12, David had a surprise visit from Nathan the prophet, who brought him a message from God. He exposed David's sin and pronounced God's judgment on him. David did not try to defend himself or make excuses but admitted, "I have sinned against the LORD" (2 Samuel 12:13). Nathan told David that God would forgive his sin but warned, "The child also who is born to you shall surely die" (v. 14).

To David's dismay, his innocent son became ill to the point of death. David pleaded to God for the child, fasting and praying all night long, but in the morning the child died. The servants were afraid to tell him, but David could tell by their demeanor that his son was dead. Second Samuel 12:20 shows David's character: "So David arose from the ground, washed and anointed himself, and changed his clothes; and he went into the house of the LORD and worshiped." He didn't become angry or blame God because he knew that this terrible tragedy in his family was a consequence of his own sin.

This experience caused David to write an emotional appeal to God that we now know as Psalm 51. David earnestly prayed, "Wash me thoroughly from my iniquity, and cleanse me from my sin. For I acknowledge my transgressions, and my sin is always before me. Against You, You only, have I sinned, and done this evil in Your sight" (Psalm 51:2-4). In order to be cleansed, David first acknowledged and confessed his sin to God. He showed a sincere regret for what he had done.

In Psalm 51:5, David wrote, "Behold, I was brought forth in iniquity, and in sin my mother conceived me." The New International Version translates this verse, "Surely I was sinful at birth, sinful from the time my mother conceived me" (NIV84). This is a gross misinterpretation of what David was saying. It suggests that a baby is sinful at birth and even *before* birth as suggested in the saying, "from the time my mother conceived me." Of course, this theory does not hold any truth. A person cannot sin until he is old enough to understand what sin is. A newborn baby is innocent and sinless.

David went on to say, "Create in me a clean heart, O God, and renew a steadfast spirit within me. Do not cast me from Your presence, and do not take Your Holy Spirit from me" (Psalm 51:10-11). David repented of his sin and asked for God's forgiveness and renewal.

Finally, David said, "Restore to me the joy of Your salvation, and uphold me by Your generous Spirit. Then I will teach transgressors Your ways, and sinners shall be converted to You" (Psalm 51:12-13).

David asked to be restored. He also learned from his mistakes and used his experience to teach others not to sin. A Christian today can also be forgiven of sin through regret, repentance, renewal and restoration. Before a person becomes a Christian, however, he must be forgiven of his sin in a different way.

## The Essential Question

On July 8, 1741, Jonathan Edwards, a Protestant preacher, preached his most famous sermon, "Sinners in the Hands of an Angry God." It could be described as a "hell fire sermon." Edwards warned his hearers that their sins made God angry, and He could throw them into hell at any time. An eyewitness, Stephen Williams, described in his diary how Edwards' words were so convincing that the sermon was interrupted many times by people moaning and crying out, "What shall I do to be saved?"

I don't know what Jonathan Edwards' answer was to that essential question, but I do know that Peter was asked a similar question on the Day of Pentecost after he preached the first gospel sermon. Acts 2:37-38 says, "Now when they heard this, they were cut to the heart, and said to Peter and the rest of the apostles, 'Men and brethren, what shall we do?' Then Peter said to them, 'Repent, and let every one of you be baptized in the name of Jesus Christ for the remission of sins; and you shall receive the gift of the Holy Spirit.' "

Baptism washes away sins, as described in Acts 22:16. When a person believes, repents of his sin, and confesses Christ, the final step to salvation is to be baptized. In Romans 6:4, Paul explains, "Therefore we were buried with Him through baptism into death, that just as Christ was raised from the dead by the glory of the Father, even so we should walk in newness of life." This is when the new Christian life begins, and the point at which we are "born again" (John 3:3). What a wonderful feeling it is to be baptized and to realize that all past sins have been washed away!

A lady who had just been baptized asked me, "Does this mean I will never sin again?" Unfortunately, the answer to that question is no. Even after a person becomes a Christian, he or she still has to deal with the sin problem. Romans 3:23 says, "For all have sinned and fall short of the glory of God." John taught, "If we say that we have no sin, we deceive ourselves, and the truth is not in us" (1 John 1:8). Within each one of us is a dark side, and Satan is eager to do anything he can to expose that side.

Paul addressed this problem by confessing his own dark side. "For the good that I will to do, I do not do, but the evil I will not to do, that I practice. Now if I do what I will not to do, it is no longer I who do it, but sin that dwells in me. ... But I see another law in my members, warring against the law in my mind, and bringing me into captivity to the law of sin which is in my members" (Romans 7:19-20, 23).

It almost sounds as if Paul is fighting a losing battle with sin, but he concludes on a positive note, "Oh wretched man that I am! Who will deliver me from this body of death? I thank God through Jesus Christ our Lord!" (Romans 7:24-25). Everyone has a propensity to sin and an internal battle going on between good and evil. Thankfully, we can overcome sin and be saved by the grace of God.

## Sin and Grace

Ephesians 2:8 teaches, "For by grace you have been saved through faith, and that not of yourselves it is the gift of God." Some people interpret this verse to mean that we don't need to do anything to be saved except believe. Others go even further and say that we can never fall from grace and that we are "once saved, always saved." This doctrine suggests that a person can continue in a life of sin and still be saved.

Paul addressed this issue in Romans 6:1-2: "What shall we say then? Shall we continue in sin that grace may abound? Certainly not! How shall we who died to sin live any longer in it?" Apparently, some of the Roman Christians had the erroneous idea that the grace of God would save them, no matter what sins they committed. The more they sinned, the more grace they would receive. Paul put a quick end to that line of thinking.

The writer of Hebrews wrote, "For it is impossible for those who were once enlightened, and have tasted the heavenly gift, and have become partakers of the Holy Spirit, and have tasted the good word of God and the powers of the age to come, if they fall away, to renew them again to repentance, since they crucify again for themselves the Son of God, and put Him to an open shame" (Hebrews 6:4-6). This verse clearly teaches that a Christian can fall away and lose his salvation.

Some Christians go to church on Sunday, worship God and seem very spiritually minded but act very differently during the rest of the week. They indulge in fornication, drunkenness, foul language and many other sins, assuming that nobody will find out about their secret lives. They may be able to fool others, but they can't fool God. James warned, "Adulterers and adulteresses! Do you not know that friendship with the world is enmity with God? Whoever therefore wants to be a friend of the world makes himself an enemy of God" (James 4:4).

Christianity is not just something we practice once a week, but it is a daily commitment. Hebrews 10:26-27 says, "For if we sin willfully after we have received the knowledge of the truth, there no longer remains a sacrifice for sins, but a certain fearful expectation of judgment, and fiery indignation which will devour the adversaries." This verse is a warning to all Christians who sin willfully. They know they are doing wrong, but they continue in sin. One day they will be held accountable to God.

All Christians sin occasionally as we saw in 1 John 1:8. John also said, "But if we walk in the light as He is in the light, we have fellowship with one another, and the blood of Jesus Christ His Son cleanses us from all sin. … If we confess our sins, He is faithful and just to forgive us our sins and to cleanse us from all unrighteousness" (vv. 7, 9). With all due respect to Jonathan Edwards, God is not an angry God just waiting for the chance to cast us all into hell. Peter wrote in 2 Peter 3:9, "The Lord is not slack concerning His promise, as some count slackness, but is longsuffering toward us, not willing that any should perish but that all should come to repentance."

## How to Battle Sin

You must first realize that you are in a battle, but it's not a physical one. It's a spiritual battle. Paul warned in Ephesians 6:12, "For we do not wrestle against flesh and blood, but against principalities, against powers, against the rulers of the darkness of this age, against spiritual hosts of wickedness in the heavenly places." In other words, we wrestle against the devil and his angels.

Peter said, "Be sober, be vigilant; because your adversary the devil walks about like a roaring lion, seeking whom he may devour" (1 Peter 5:8). He cannot speak to you audibly as he did to Eve, but he will use your thoughts, your circumstances and other people to lure you into sin. However, there are things you can do to win the battle against Satan.

• **Keep Your Thoughts Pure**. James gives a suggestion for a twofold punch against the devil. First he says, "Resist the devil and he will flee from you" (James 4:7). Don't associate with people who will invite you to do things that you know are wrong. Stay away from anything that will cause you to lust, have evil thoughts or do evil deeds. That can mean avoiding some movies, TV shows, books or Internet sites that promote sinful practices. James also said, "But each one is tempted when he is drawn away by his own desires and enticed. Then, when desire has conceived, it gives birth to sin; and sin, when it is full-grown, brings forth death" (1:14-15). Sin begins in the mind. That's why it is important to keep your thoughts pure. When an evil or lustful thought comes into your mind, stop the desire before it leads to sin and death.

As Paul said in 2 Corinthians 11:14, "For Satan himself transforms himself into an angel of light." Just as he deceived Eve into thinking that disobeying God would make her wise, Satan will try to make sin look attractive. It's cool, and everyone else is doing it, so why not you? Don't listen to the devil's lies.

• **Draw Near to God**. The second part of James' twofold punch is in James 4:8, "Draw near to God and He will draw near to you." It's not enough just to resist the devil. You must also draw near to God. Spend quality time in Bible study and prayer. Make worship a regular practice, not just on Sunday morning but all the services if you are able. Have fellowship with other Christians who have the same values as you.

• **Get to Know the Bible**. Satan was so brazen that he thought he could even tempt Jesus to sin. In Matthew 4:1-11, Jesus was approached by the devil three times with three different temptations. Each time, Jesus answered by first saying, "It is written." He quoted scriptures to counter Satan's attacks.

Paul advised the Ephesian Christians to use the whole armor of God when fighting against the devil. He said to take "the sword of the Spirit, which is the word of God" (Ephesians 6:17). To battle against Satan, you need to have your sword ready at all times. You need to know the Word and be familiar with its teachings. David said in Psalm 119:11, "Your word I have hidden in my heart, that I might not sin against You."

Flip Wilson had a popular comedy show in the 1970s in which he portrayed many colorful characters, one of whom was Geraldine. She was a somewhat confused young woman who was always getting into some minor mishap. Her excuse for her behavior was always the same, "The devil made me do it!" The truth is the devil can't *make* you do anything. You choose whether to sin or not to sin. However, if you keep walking in the light, Satan will not be able to turn you over to the dark side.

## Questions to Ponder

1. What three methods did Satan use to deceive Eve (Genesis 3:1-7)?
2. What were some conditions that contributed to David's sin that escalated into more sins (2 Samuel 11:1-17)?
3. What was David's response when Nathan the prophet confronted him with his sin (2 Samuel 12:7-23)?
4. How are our sins washed away (Acts 2:38; 22:16)?
5. What will happen to a person who calls himself a Christian but continually and willfully lives a life of sin (Hebrews 10:26-27)?
6. In what ways do the media (movies, TV shows, books, Internet) make sin look attractive and acceptable?
7. What was James' twofold punch against sin in James 4:7-8?

# The Prince of Darkness

*Just as a roaring lion, seeking whom he may devour,*
*The devil comes to tempt you any day or any hour.*
*He is cunning, he is crafty, always trying to deceive*
*As he did back in the Garden with the unsuspecting Eve.*
*He is called the Prince of Darkness and the Father of all Lies.*
*He can even try to tempt you as an angel in disguise.*
*But don't give in to the devil as he tries to make you sin.*
*He will fight to take control, but you don't have to let him win.*
*Although he has some power, he is really cowardly.*
*He knows when he's defeated. Just resist him, and he'll flee.*
*While the devil is like darkness, Jesus Christ is our true Light.*
*Keep walking close to Jesus, and He will keep you right.*

# The Word on Sin

**Psalm 119:11**

"Your word I have hidden in my heart,
that I might not sin against You."

**Hebrews 12:1**

"Let us lay aside every weight, and the sin which so easily ensnares us, and let us run with endurance the race that is set before us."

**James 4:7-8**

"Therefore submit to God. Resist the devil and he will flee from you. Draw near to God and He will draw near to you."

**1 John 1:7**

"But if we walk in the light as He is in the light,
we have fellowship with one another, and the blood of
Jesus Christ His Son cleanses us from all sin."

Chapter 6

# Persistent Sadness

## *Depression*

Solomon wrote in Proverbs 17:22, "A merry heart does good, like medicine, but a broken spirit dries the bones." Many people today think the only way to gain a merry heart is from a medicine bottle. According to research from Dr. Joseph Mercola's newsletter, 230 million prescriptions for antidepressants are filled every year in the United States alone. The number of people taking these drugs doubled in one decade, from 13.3 million in 1997 to 27 million in 2005. Depression has become an epidemic in America and around the world.

Although the symptoms can vary, depending on whether a person is suffering from minor, moderate or severe depression, the Mayo Clinic lists these common symptoms.

- Feelings of sadness or unhappiness
- Irritability or frustration, even over minor matters, angry outbursts
- Loss of interest or pleasure in normal activities
- Reduced sex drive
- Insomnia or excessive sleep
- Changes in appetite – either decreased or increased
- Agitation or restlessness – for example, pacing, hand-wringing or an inability to sit still
- Slowed thinking, speaking or body movements
- Indecisiveness, distractibility and decreased concentration

• Fatigue, tiredness and loss of energy – even small tasks may seem to require a lot of effort
• Feelings of worthlessness or guilt, blaming yourself when things aren't going right
• Trouble thinking, concentrating, making decisions and remembering things
• Frequent thoughts of death, dying or suicide
• Crying spells for no apparent reason
• Unexplained physical problems, such as back pain or headache.

Depression can be caused by many factors, such as stress at home or at work, grief from loss of a loved one, worry, chronic pain, hormonal changes, health conditions and even genetics. Usually, it is not just one thing, but a combination of factors that can lead to depression. Understanding the cause can be the first step to overcoming the condition.

## Hannah's Heartache

Like many women, Hannah longed to have a baby. Her husband's other wife Peninnah had children, but Hannah had none, which made her very sad. To make matters worse, Peninnah taunted her mercilessly as described in 1 Samuel 1:6-7: "And her rival also provoked her severely, to make her miserable, because the LORD had closed her womb. So it was, year by year, when she went up to the house of the LORD, that she provoked her; therefore she wept and did not eat."

Hannah showed some of the classic signs of depression. She was miserable. She would not eat. She could not stop crying. "She was in bitterness of soul, and prayed to the LORD and wept in anguish" (1 Samuel 1:10). Her husband, Elkanah, loved her very much and tried to comfort her with these words, "Hannah, why do you weep? Why do you not eat? And why is your heart grieved? Am I not better to you than ten sons?" (v. 8). His attitude was, "Why are you sad when you have me?"

Elkanah meant well and was sincerely trying to help. Like most men, he felt that if there was a problem he would be able to fix it. But a man cannot understand a woman's deep desire for a child and the heartache that infertility can cause. When people are depressed by circumstances beyond their control, telling them to "cheer up" or "snap out of it" only makes them feel worse.

When Hannah was in the tabernacle, the place of worship, she poured out her heart to the Lord in prayer. Eli, the priest, misunderstood her body language and accused her of being drunk! Hannah explained that she was not drunk but was a "woman of sorrowful spirit" (1 Samuel 1:15), and "out of the abundance of my complaint and grief I have spoken until now" (v. 16). Eli told her the Lord would grant her petition.

Immediately after hearing those reassuring words, Hannah "went her way and ate, and her face was no longer sad" (1 Samuel 1:18). Her faith was so great that even before her prayer was answered, she believed the promise and was full of joy once again. Hannah's faith was rewarded when she gave birth to a son and named him Samuel which means "heard by God." Later she was blessed even more with three sons and two daughters (1 Samuel 2:21).

The wise King Solomon wrote in Proverbs 13:12, "Hope deferred makes the heart sick, but when the desire comes, it is a tree of life." This was true in Hannah's case. Her heart was sick because of an unfulfilled hope, but once the desire was realized she was cured of her depression.

## Elijah's Escape

Although women seem to suffer from depression twice as much as men, the statistics can be misleading. Men are also prone to depression, but the symptoms can be very different. Whereas women tend to be sad and weepy, men are more likely to manifest their depression with anger and irritability. Men often avoid talking about their feelings of anxiety; consequently the condition can go undetected and untreated.

Elijah was a great prophet of God. He was a tough, no-nonsense kind of guy who showed no fear in confronting the powerful King Ahab. In 1 Kings 18, Elijah challenged 400 prophets of Baal to a contest to see who was the true God. Although he won an overwhelming victory against the prophets of Baal and had all of them executed, Elijah felt powerless against one woman – the wicked Queen Jezebel. She sent a message telling Elijah, "So let the gods do to me, and more also, if I do not make your life as the life of one of them by tomorrow about this time" (1 Kings 19:2).

Elijah immediately escaped to the wilderness where he prayed, "It is enough! Now, LORD, take my life, for I am no better than my fathers!"

(1 Kings 19:4). Elijah was so depressed that he wanted to die. He did not have the strength to go on with his work or even with his life. This response is not unusual. An online fact sheet by Dr. Bob Murray revealed that men typically develop depression in their 40s and 50s, as they begin to reach retirement age. The suicide rate among men in this age group is three times the U.S. national average. An even more disturbing statistic is that 80 percent of all suicides are men.

As Elijah languished in the wilderness under a broom tree, he was visited by an angel who came to strengthen him. First Kings 19:6 says, "Then he looked, and there by his head was a cake baked on coals, and a jar of water. So he ate and drank, and lay down again." Food can be very comforting. It may have helped Elijah somewhat, but it wasn't enough. He lay down again. He still had no energy or enthusiasm for life.

God spoke in a "still small voice" and gave Elijah the opportunity to talk about how he felt (1 Kings 19:12). Elijah explained, "I have been very zealous for the LORD God of hosts; because the children of Israel have forsaken Your covenant, torn down Your altars, and killed Your prophets with the sword. I alone am left; and they seek to take my life" (1 Kings 19:14). Elijah's depression was caused by a feeling of hopelessness. He felt all alone. He wondered if his work had been in vain and if all he had done had been worth the effort.

God did two things for Elijah. First, He gave him a job to do. God gave Elijah the assignment of anointing Hazael as king over Syria and Jehu as king over Israel. He was telling Elijah that his work was not over just yet. There was still more to be done. Elijah also was told that he was not alone because God had "reserved seven thousand in Israel, all whose knees have not bowed to Baal, and every mouth that has not kissed him" (1 Kings 19:18).

Second, God gave him a friend to be a helper and encourager. From that time on, Elijah became the mentor of Elisha, who eventually succeeded him as prophet of Israel. The work of Elijah did continue. He regained his strength and enthusiasm. One day as he was walking along with Elisha, a wonderful thing happened as recorded in 2 Kings 2:11: "Then it happened, as they continued on and talked, that suddenly a chariot of fire appeared with horses of fire, and separated the two of them; and Elijah went up by a whirlwind into heaven." Elijah received the ultimate reward – heaven, a place where he would never again be plagued by depression.

## No Apparent Reason

Both Hannah and Elijah were able to overcome their depression when the cause of their sadness was resolved. Hannah had the children she so desperately wanted. Elijah found meaning and purpose in his work once again. Proverbs 12:25 wisely teaches, "Anxiety in the heart of man causes depression, but a good word makes it glad."

Many people, however, are depressed for no apparent reason. Their sadness is not caused by a specific circumstance or stressful time. They really don't know why they have such low feelings. One lady confided to me, "When I burst into tears because I dropped a spoon on the floor, I knew I needed to get help."

Depression is often caused by a chemical imbalance in the brain, especially low doses of serotonin, norepinephrine and dopamine. This can be corrected with the right dosage of antidepressant medication. Keep in mind that many of these medications have dangerous side effects. A good doctor will try different medicines until he finds the one that works best for you and will start off with a low dosage. Ideally, these drugs should be used for a short time and should be tapered off as the condition improves.

Other physical ailments that can cause depression are thyroid disease, diabetes, Parkinson's disease, dementia, multiple sclerosis, heart disease and even dehydration. A person with unexplained depression should get a complete physical done by a doctor to check for some of these conditions. Spending regular time with The Great Physician will also be a tremendous benefit. William Hunter, a 19th-century hymnist, wrote, "The great Physician now is near, The sympathizing Jesus; He speaks the drooping heart to cheer: O hear the voice of Jesus."

## How to Cope With Depression

• **Spend Some Time in the Sun**. Dr. Joseph Mercola, who specializes in alternative medicine, has written that a deficiency in Vitamin D can lead to depression. He recommends a Vitamin D supplement, as well as adequate sun exposure. Other natural remedies, such as fish oil pills with Omega-3 and St. John's Wort, can help to alleviate depression. People who suffer from Seasonal Affective Disorder (SAD) during the winter months because of the longer dark nights have often found relief from light therapy.

• **Communicate Your Feelings**. If you are feeling depressed because of the daily struggles and problems of life, it would help to talk it out with a friend. It may be necessary to speak to a therapist or counselor who can help you resolve inner conflicts. Keeping negative feelings pent up for a long period of time can be harmful and can even lead to heart disease, ulcers and other disorders. It's amazing how much better you feel after talking about your feelings to someone who will listen and care.

• **Communicate With God**. If you don't have anyone you feel comfortable sharing a confidence with, you can always talk to God. Peter says in 1 Peter 5:7 that you should be "casting all your care upon Him, for He cares for you." Paul said, "Rejoice always, pray without ceasing" (1 Thessalonians 5:16-17). Communication with God involves not only talking (prayer), but also listening (reading God's Word). Couple your prayer time with Bible reading. Look up verses about joy and rejoicing, and think about those verses whenever you are feeling sad. One verse that is easy to remember is Philippians 4:4 – "Rejoice in the Lord always. Again I will say, rejoice!"

• **Keep a Journal**. If you are a person who feels more comfortable writing than talking, you may benefit from keeping a feelings journal. Have a special notebook that you keep just to write down how you feel and why you are feeling that way. Writing down all your feelings can be as therapeutic as talking about them. Going back later to read what you wrote can help you understand yourself better and see patterns that trigger depression.

• **Exercise**. Studies have shown that exercise can alleviate depression. Most people don't enjoy strenuous exercise or working out, but after it is over they feel so much better and stronger. Taking a walk outside and enjoying the beauty of nature has a calming effect. When you feel calm and relaxed, you feel more joyful.

• **Volunteer**. I read in a magazine that volunteering is a good way to alleviate depression. I decided to test that theory and signed up to do some volunteer work at the local hospital. I can attest that it really works. Volunteering just gives you a good feeling because you know you are helping someone else.

• **Think Positive Thoughts**. One of the main causes of depression is negative thinking. When you are depressed, you think everything is going wrong, nobody cares, things will never get better, and the list goes on and on. When you are in one of those negative moods, it's hard to switch into a positive spirit, but it can be done. You may have to force yourself to change your thought pattern. Instead of thinking negative thoughts, make a conscious effort to think positive thoughts. Norman Vincent Peale had some very good advice on the subject. One of his suggestions was to practice visualization. Visualize in your mind all your problems, fears and frustrations as an army in front of you. Then imagine that army retreating as you tell them to go away. Paul wrote about positive thinking in Philippians 4:8. "Finally, brethren, whatever things are true, whatever things are noble, whatever things are just, whatever things are pure, whatever things are lovely, whatever things are of good report, if there is any virtue and if there is anything praiseworthy – meditate on these things."

• **Sing Happy Songs**. Music is a great mood enhancer. Listen to some good, cheerful songs. Better yet, sing at the top of your voice, even if you are by yourself! It's hard to be sad while singing "Sing and Be Happy Today."

• **Be Thankful**. When you are feeling depressed, think of all the things that you are thankful for, even the little things. Paul said in 1 Thessalonians 5:18, "In everything give thanks; for this is the will of God in Christ Jesus for you." He also said in Philippians 4:6. "Be anxious for nothing, but in everything by prayer and supplication, with thanksgiving, let your requests be made known to God." Notice we are to be thankful, not just when things are going well, but even when we are going through anxiety. Take time to thank God every day, and also show gratitude to all the people who have been a blessing to you.

If you have many of the symptoms of depression consistently for more than two weeks, you should seek professional help. If you struggle with depression off and on, some of these suggestions may help you to feel happier. Remember Psalm 30:5: "Weeping may endure for a night, but joy comes in the morning."

## Questions to Ponder

1. In what ways did Hannah show symptoms of depression? What was the cause of her depression (1 Samuel 1:6-18)?
2. Why did Elijah want to die (1 Kings 19:4, 14)?
3. What did God do to help Elijah recover from his depressed spirit (1 Kings 19: 15-21)?
4. How does depression affect men and women differently?
5. What are some things that cheer you up when you are in a sad mood?
6. How does a thankful spirit help a person who is feeling depressed?
7. How does negative thinking cause depression?

# Depression

*Depression bears upon me like a mighty, crushing weight.*
*I can't remember simple things; I just can't concentrate.*
*I feel persistent sadness that reduces me to tears.*
*My mind is filled with anxious thoughts with many doubts and fears.*
*I have no energy for things I used to love to do.*
*Some days I want to stay in bed and sleep the whole day through.*
*But God sees all my sorrow, and I know He's always there*
*To heal me as I pray and cast on Him my every care.*

# The Word on Depression

**Psalm 118:2**

"This is the day the LORD has made;
we will rejoice and be glad in it."

**Proverbs 12:25**

"Anxiety in the heart of man causes depression,
but a good word makes it glad."

**Philippians 4:4**

"Rejoice in the Lord always. Again I will say, rejoice!"

**1 Thessalonians 5:16-18**

"Rejoice always, pray without ceasing, in everything give thanks;
for this is the will of God in Christ Jesus for you."

Chapter 7

# A Heavy Burden

## *Guilt*

Court is in session. The jury has made its decision. The defendant watches nervously as the foreman stands up to give the verdict. The silence in the courtroom is shattered as the verdict is revealed, "Guilty!"

No one likes to be declared guilty, but everyone is guilty of something, whether it's a major crime or a minor unkind thought. Guilt can actually be a good thing. A man once got a mysterious package in the mail with $500 in cash and an anonymous note from someone who had stolen the money from him many years ago. The perpetrator's guilty conscience caused him or her to repent and make restitution.

A guilty conscience can also prevent a person from doing an evil deed. In John 8, some men brought a woman who had been caught in the very act of adultery to Jesus and said, "Now Moses, in the law, commanded us that such should be stoned. But what do You say?" (John 8:5). Jesus said that whoever was without sin should cast the first stone. "Then those who heard it, being convicted by their conscience, went out one by one, beginning from the oldest even to the last" (v. 9). No one wanted to be the first one to cast the stone because their conscience told them they were all guilty of sin.

The Greek word for "conscience" literally means "to be one's own witness." Someone has said that our conscience is the little voice inside our head that tells us what is right and wrong. A song from the movie *Pinocchio* advised, "Always let your conscience be your guide." But is that good advice? Paul warned Timothy that some would depart from the faith, "having their own conscience seared with a hot iron" (1 Timothy 4:1-2). Our conscience is not always reliable. We should pay attention to that inner voice, but the best advice is to let God's Word be our guide.

Some people deal with their guilt by blaming someone else. Others try to deny any wrongdoing. Sadly, many people deal with guilt by blaming themselves. They struggle for years with the burden of guilt from past sins or even from things that were not their fault. A teenager commits suicide, and his parents blame themselves for not noticing the signs and being able to prevent it. Any sin or mistake from the past can prick a person's conscience. Intense feelings of guilt can cause depression and, in some cases, even lead to suicide.

## Two Apostles; Two Different Outcomes

Although he had followed Jesus for three years, listened to His teachings and seen the miracles, Judas Iscariot plotted with the Pharisees to turn Jesus over to them for 30 pieces of silver. His chance came after he left the last supper that he shared with Jesus and the other apostles. On that fateful night, Judas went to Gethsemane with a multitude of armed men, and with a kiss of betrayal, led them straight to Jesus (Matthew 26:47-49).

The very next day, Judas had a totally different attitude. Matthew tells us, "When morning came, all the chief priests and elders of the people plotted against Jesus to put Him to death. … Then Judas, His betrayer, seeing that He had been condemned, was remorseful and brought back the thirty pieces of silver to the chief priests and elders, saying, 'I have sinned by betraying innocent blood.' And they said, 'What is that to us? You see to it!' " (Matthew 27:1, 3-4). Perhaps Judas assumed that Jesus would be arrested and later released. When he realized the consequences of his betrayal, Judas was remorseful and tried to make restitution by giving the money back, but the chief priests would not accept it. Unable to bear the magnitude of his guilt, Judas threw the money down, and then hanged himself (v. 5).

In a sense, Peter also betrayed Jesus because he denied he even knew

Him. Just before going to Gethsemane, Jesus warned Peter this would happen, but Peter vehemently declared that even if he had to die with Jesus, he would not deny Him (Matthew 26:34-35).

Later that evening, when Peter was asked on three different occasions if he had been with Jesus, he denied that he knew Him each time. Luke records that after the third denial "the Lord turned and looked at Peter. Then Peter remembered the word of the Lord, how He had said to him, 'Before the rooster crows, you will deny Me three times.' So Peter went out and wept bitterly" (Luke 22:61-62). Like Judas, Peter was also remorseful for what he had done. He had been one of Jesus' closest friends making the denial even worse. Unlike Judas though, Peter had the opportunity to see Jesus after He had been raised from the dead as recorded in John 20:19, 24-26 and Luke 24:33-34.

After these appearances by Jesus, Peter told some of the other disciples, "I am going fishing" (John 21:3). Some Bible scholars suggest that Peter decided to give up the idea of being a fisher of men to go back to being a lowly fisherman. This is another tactic that some people use to deal with feelings of guilt. Putting all their energy into work or other projects can temporarily ease their emotional pain. Staying busy helps them to forget the pangs of guilt. Peter's influence on the other disciples was clearly seen when they all said, "We are going with you also." They fished all night but caught nothing.

The next morning, Jesus stood on the shore, telling them to cast their nets on the right side of the boat. Then they caught a whole multitude of fish (John 21:11). Jesus invited the disciples to come have some fish for breakfast. As they ate, Jesus asked Peter, "Simon, son of Jonah, do you love Me more than these?" Peter answered, "Yes, Lord; You know that I love You." Jesus asked the same question, "Do you love Me?", a second time and then a third time (vv. 15-17). John 21:17 says that "Peter was grieved because He said to him the third time, 'Do you love me?' "

Although the question caused Peter pain, it was a question that needed to be asked. Peter was given the chance to reaffirm his love for Jesus. Just as Peter denied Jesus three times, now he was affirming Jesus three times. The Lord also gave him a mission: "Feed My sheep." He was reassuring Peter that although he had made a mistake, he was still useful in His service. Peter went on to preach the first gospel sermon on the Day of Pentecost, the day that 3,000 people were baptized and added to the church (Acts 2:14- 41). He was a strong and faithful leader in the church until the day he died.

Peter and Judas both wrestled with guilt, but the outcome for each of them was entirely different. Judas could have repented and been forgiven, but he looked back at his sin and focused on his own guilt and shame. Peter struggled with guilt, but he decided to focus on Jesus and go forward with a renewed commitment. Judas ended his life with tragedy while Peter finished his life in triumph.

## "I Feel So Unworthy"

We saw in an earlier chapter how Joseph's brothers sold him into slavery out of jealousy. Many years later, when the brothers went to Egypt to buy food, they encountered a harsh Egyptian ruler, not realizing that he was their long lost little brother. After Joseph accused them of being spies, the brothers said to one another, "We are truly guilty concerning our brother, for we saw the anguish of his soul when he pleaded with us, and we would not hear; therefore this distress has come upon us" (Genesis 42:21). The brothers had gone on with their lives after their sin against Joseph, but even 20 years later, the guilt of what they had done still pricked their conscience. They acknowledged that their present struggles were punishment for their evil deed.

Joseph later revealed his true identity to his brothers and invited them all to come to Egypt. After so many years, Joseph was overjoyed to be reunited with his father, Jacob. Jacob lived in Egypt 17 years according to Genesis 47:28. After Jacob died, Joseph's brothers reasoned among themselves, "Perhaps Joseph will hate us, and will actually repay us for all the evil which we did to him" (Genesis 50:15). They sent a message to Joseph, begging for his forgiveness, even though he had already forgiven them 17 years before. Many people have those same doubts about God. They ask for God's forgiveness for past sins, but then wonder if they are really forgiven. One elderly Christian lady confided to me that she sometimes doubted her salvation because she had done so many bad things before she became a Christian. When I pointed out that those sins were forgiven when she was baptized, she said, "Yes, I know, but sometimes I feel so unworthy."

In Jesus' parable of the prodigal son, the boy who wasted all his money on prodigal living finally "came to himself" and made some tough decisions. He decided to go back to his father and say, "Father, I have sinned against heaven and before you, and I am no longer worthy to be called your son. Make me like one of your hired servants" (Luke 15:17-19). When he got home, his rehearsed speech was interrupted by his joyful father calling for a feast to celebrate his son's return. The son was forgiven, not because he was worthy, but because the father was loving and merciful. The father in Jesus' story represents our Father in heaven. Jesus said, "There will be more joy in heaven over one sinner who repents than over ninety-nine just persons who need no repentance" (Luke 15:7).

In the book of Revelation, John saw a glorious vision of angels and elders in heaven asking, "Who is worthy to open the scroll and to loose its seals?" Then John saw "a Lamb as though it had been slain" who took the scroll, causing the elders to sing, "You are worthy to take the scroll, and to open its seals; for You were slain, and have redeemed us to God by Your blood." Then John heard thousands of angels saying, "Worthy is the Lamb who was slain to receive power and riches and wisdom, and strength and honor and glory and blessing!" (Revelation 5:1-12).

All of us have sinned, as Paul said in Romans 3:23. None of us are really worthy, but Jesus is worthy because He is "the Lamb of God who takes away the sin of the world" (John 1:29). Because of the sacrifice of Jesus, we can be free from the guilt of sin.

## How to Overcome Guilt

• **Turn Away From Sin**. First of all, if you are feeling guilty because of some unrepented sin, then you *should* feel guilty. Your conscience is working to convict you of your sin. If you are not a Christian, you need to believe in Jesus, repent of your sins, confess that Jesus is the Son of God, and be baptized for the remission of sins (Acts 2:38). Then your sins will be washed away (22:16). You will then need to turn away from sin and live a righteous life in Christ.

If you are a Christian and are continuing to live a sinful lifestyle, you need to turn from that sin and ask God to forgive you (1 John 1:9). If you are guilty of a public sin that is known by many people, you should confess your sin, as James commanded: "Confess your trespasses to one another, and pray for one another, that you may be healed. The effective, fervent prayer of a righteous man avails much" (James 5:16).

• **Make Restitution**. If you are guilty of a sin that has affected other people, such as lying or stealing, you might need to make some form of restitution. If you have stolen money or possessions, you need to pay back what you have taken. If you have lied about someone and slandered her reputation, you should do all you can to restore her reputation. If you have said angry words to someone and now regret your outburst, go to her as soon as possible to apologize and make amends.

• **Examine Yourself**. Some people feel a sense of guilt and unworthiness and are not even sure why they feel that way. If you tend to have those feelings, read David's prayer in Psalm 139:23-24: "Search me, O God, and know my heart; try me, and know my anxieties; and see if there is any wicked way in me, and lead me in the way everlasting." Say that prayer and sincerely examine yourself. If you find some sin in your heart, repent of it and ask God for forgiveness. Each night before you go to bed, ask God to forgive all your sins. If you know of any wrongdoing or bad thought, pray for each one specifically.

• **Be Careful of Guilt by Association**. A 21-year-old man who was between jobs was grateful when a casual acquaintance offered him money to deliver a package. Unknown to him, he was actually part of a drug deal. The person at the address was an undercover policeman, who immediately arrested him. The young man spent several months in jail, even though the crime he was involved in was done in ignorance.

In another incident, a teenager went to a party where there was underage drinking. An anonymous tip led police to raid the party. Although the teenager had not participated in the drinking, he was questioned along with the other offenders. Everyone, especially young people, need to know exactly what kind of people they are associating with. "Do not be deceived: 'Evil company corrupts good habits' " (1 Corinthians 15:33).

• **Believe in Forgiveness**. When you ask for God's forgiveness, believe that He has truly forgiven you. In her book, *Tramp for the Lord*, Corrie ten Boom quoted from Micah 7:19, "You will cast all our sins into the depths of the sea." She then added that God takes all our sins and throws them into the sea of forgetfulness and then puts up a sign that says, "No Fishing." Her point was that you don't need to go back to your past sins that God has already forgiven and try to bring them up again. God spoke through the prophet, Jeremiah, "I will forgive their iniquity, and their sin I will remember no more" (Jeremiah 31:34). If God does not remember the sins from your past, then neither should you.

A young girl who was given a ticket for a traffic violation stood before the judge asking for his mercy. He shook his head and told her she was guilty and the fine would have to be paid. Then he took off his judge's robe, stood beside her and paid the fine. He was her judge, but he was also her father. God is our Judge, but He is also our Father, and He has paid for our sins with the blood of Jesus. The writer of Hebrews asked, "For if the blood of bulls and goats and the ashes of a heifer, sprinkling the unclean, sanctifies for the purifying of the flesh, how much more shall the blood of Christ, who through the eternal Spirit offered Himself without spot to God, cleanse your conscience from dead works to serve the living God?" (Hebrews 9:13-14).

## Questions to Ponder

1. What is a conscience, and how does it help us in our daily lives?

2. What do you think caused Judas to be remorseful for betraying Jesus? How did he try to make restitution (Matthew 27:1-5)?

3. What did Judas' burden of guilt cause him to do? Do you think he could have repented and been forgiven by God and the other apostles?

4. What was Peter's sin? How did he show remorse for his denial (Luke 22:61-62)?

5. How did Jesus help Peter to overcome his feelings of guilt (John 21:1-19)?

6. Why do some people feel unworthy because of their past sins?

7. What is meant by Corrie ten Boom's phrase, "God takes our sins and throws them into the sea of forgetfulness, and then puts up a sign that says 'No fishing'"?

# I Forgive You

*Burdened with guilt, I cried out in despair,*
*"Father, forgive me, and please hear my prayer."*
*"Yes, I forgive you," God said lovingly.*
*"Your sins have been cast in the depths of the sea."*
*But still I had doubts, so I prayed once again,*
*"Lord, please forgive me of this terrible sin."*
*And then in a voice so kind and so tender,*
*God asked, "What sin? I don't remember."*

# The Word on Guilt

**Isaiah 1:18**

"Come now and let us reason together," says the LORD,
"Though your sins are like scarlet, they shall be as snow;
though they are red like crimson, they shall be as wool."

**Isaiah 43:25**

"I, even I, am He who blots out your transgressions for
My own sake; and I will not remember your sins."

**Acts 24:16**

"This being so, I myself always strive to have a conscience
without offense toward God and men."

**Philippians 3:13-14**

"Brethren, I do not count myself to have apprehended; but one thing I do, forgetting those things which are behind and reaching forward to those things which are ahead, I press toward the goal for the prize of the upward call of God in Christ Jesus."

Chapter 8

# Danger Without the "D"

## *Anger*

We often sing a hymn that says, "Angry words! O let them never From the tongue unbridled slip; May the heart's best impulse ever Check them ere they soil the lip" (Horatio Palmer). Anger begins with a thought. Angry thoughts lead to angry words and actions.

In Genesis 4:4-8, Cain was angry because the offering of his brother, Abel, was accepted by God, and his was not. God said to Cain, "Why are you angry? And why has your countenance fallen? If you do well, will you not be accepted? And if you do not do well, sin lies at the door. And its desire is for you, but you should rule over it." God was warning Cain that anger could lead to sin and he needed to master it. Instead of heeding God's advice, Cain's uncontrolled anger led to the very first murder. The same warning applies to us today. If we do not control our angry feelings, then anger will control us.

### Don't Be Cruel

Not everyone deals with anger in the same way. Some people become enraged and quickly lose their temper, ranting and raving at whoever happens to raise their ire. Genesis 27 tells about Esau's anger toward his twin brother, Jacob, for stealing the blessing that rightly belonged to Esau. He was so angry that he threatened to kill Jacob. Their mother, Rebekah, advised Jacob to go to her brother in Haran "and stay with him for a few days … until your brother's anger turns away from you, and he forgets what you have done to him" (vv. 44-45). The "few days" turned into 20 years. After all that time in Haran, Jacob returned to his homeland with his two wives, two concubines, 11 sons and one daughter. He was afraid to meet Esau again, but he was literally welcomed back with open arms. Over the years, Esau's anger had subsided, and he was able to forgive his brother (33:3-4).

Jacob settled his family in a city called Shechem (Genesis 33:18). His sons became angry when Shechem, the prince of the country, violated their sister, Dinah (34:1-7). Two of Jacob's sons, Simeon and Levi, killed all the males in Shechem's family with the sword (vv. 25-26). Many years later, when Jacob lay dying in Egypt, he gathered all his sons together to give them their blessing. He said, "Simeon and Levi are brothers; instruments of cruelty are in their dwelling place. … Cursed be their anger, for it is fierce; and their wrath, for it is cruel!" (49:5, 7).

Anger can cause a person to be cruel. Cruelty can be manifested not only through violence but through mean and hurtful words that can leave permanent emotional scars. Solomon spoke against this kind of anger in Proverbs. He advised, "Make no friendship with an angry man, and with a furious man do not go, lest you learn his ways and set a snare for your soul" (Proverbs 22:24-25). He also said, "An angry man stirs up strife, and a furious man abounds in transgression" (29:22).

Paul warned in Colossians 3:8, "But now you yourselves are to put off all these: anger, wrath, malice." Anger is a stepping stone to wrath, which means "forceful vindictive anger." Wrath leads to malice, defined as "a desire to harm others." We may become angry when provoked, but that does not give us the right to hurt someone else.

Jesus taught in the Sermon on the Mount, "But I say to you that whoever is angry with his brother without a cause shall be in danger of the judgment. And whoever says to his brother, 'Raca!' shall be in danger of the council. But whoever says, 'You fool!' shall be in danger of hell fire" (Matthew 5:22). Warren Wiersbe explained that "Raca" means, "Empty-headed person" (23). He wrote in his commentary on this passage, "Anger is such a foolish thing. It makes us destroyers instead of builders. It robs us of freedom and makes us prisoners. To hate someone is to commit murder in our hearts" (23).

## Repressed Anger

Some people turn their anger inward. Instead of losing their tempers, they keep their anger bottled up inside them. Most people are familiar with the story of Jonah, the prophet who was swallowed by a great fish because he disobeyed God's command to preach to the people of Nineveh. Finally, he did preach in Nineveh, and all the people repented and believed in God. Most preachers would be happy for such a revival, but Jonah 4:1 says, "But it displeased Jonah exceedingly, and he became angry."

Jonah was angry because he wanted to see the wicked people of Nineveh destroyed. He told God to take his life because it was better to die than to live. The Lord asked him, "Is it right for you to be angry?" (Jonah 4:3-4). Jonah turned his anger inward and became depressed. He preferred to die, rather than deal with his anger. This is a common symptom of repressed anger. Dr. Paul Meier, psychiatrist and co-founder of the Minirth-Meier Clinics, wrote that 95 percent of all cases of depression are caused by repressed anger toward an abuser or toward oneself (168). Comedian Steven Wright once said that depression is just anger without all the enthusiasm.

Jonah apparently thought God might change His mind about judgment against Nineveh. He sat down "till he might see what would become of the city" (Jonah 4:5). While he sat watching the city, God prepared a plant to grow over his head and give him shade from the sun. The next day, God caused the plant to wither. With no protection from the blazing sun, Jonah grew faint and once again said, "It is better for me to die than to live" (vv. 6-8).

God asked Jonah, "Is it right for you to be angry about the plant?" Jonah answered, "It is right for me to be angry, even to death!" (Jonah 4:9). Jonah claimed to be angry about the plant when he was really angry at God and the Ninevites. People who suppress their anger don't talk about what has made them angry. The problem with hidden anger is that it will come out in other ways. A man is angry because a co-worker berated him; then he goes home and criticizes his wife. The wife is angry about the husband's criticism and nags him about coming home late. They start to argue about everything except the real cause of their anger.

Anger that is hidden inside for a long period of time can sometimes lead to tragedy. After a school or workplace shooting rampage, people will often show surprise because the perpetrator seemed like such a quiet, unassuming person. Dr. Paul Meier wrote in his book, *Don't Let Jerks Get the Best of You*, "Actually, explosive anger that involves shouting, screaming and even hitting is not as dangerous in the long run as repressed anger. The person who explodes gets over it and cools off. But the person who stuffs his anger does not get over it. He thinks he's fine, when in truth, he's a walking time bomb" (177).

## Absalom's Anger

An example from the Bible of this kind of anger is found in the story of Absalom. Absalom was angry at his brother Amnon for raping his sister Tamar. According to 2 Samuel 13:22, "Absalom spoke to his brother Amnon neither good nor bad. For Absalom hated Amnon because he had forced his sister Tamar." The next few verses say that after two full years had passed, Absalom politely asked his father, David, if Amnon and his other brothers could go to a sheepshearing event. David granted permission, never suspecting that Absalom had murder on his mind. While they were gone, Absalom commanded his servants to kill Amnon (vv. 23-29). After two years of letting his anger seethe, he finally got revenge. Then Absalom fled to Geshur where he stayed for three years (v. 38).

In 2 Samuel 14, Joab and a wise woman of Tekoa persuaded David to bring Absalom back to Jerusalem. Absalom had been banished for three years. Even after he came back to Jerusalem, he still did not see his own father until after another two years (2 Samuel 14:28). Absalom finally did have a reunion with David, but he still had anger issues. His anger had shifted from his brother to his father. He used his good looks and charm to win over the people and to try to take over David's kingdom. David had to flee for his life from his own son. In the end, Absalom was killed in battle, causing David to lament, "O my son, Absalom – my son, my son Absalom – if only I had died in your place! O Absalom my son, my son" (18:33).

No one could see the signs of anger that lurked inside Absalom's heart. According to 2 Samuel 15:6, "Absalom stole the hearts of the men of Israel." He seemed so charming and sincere on the outside, but his inner anger brought tragedy, division and heartbreak to David's family.

## Righteous Anger

Paul admonished Christians in Ephesians 4:26, "'Be angry, and do not sin': do not let the sun go down on your wrath." It is possible to be angry and not sin. Anger can be channeled into something good.

On May 3, 1980, Candice Lightner's 13-year-old daughter was killed by a hit and run drunk driver. Mrs. Lightner was not only grief-stricken because of her daughter's death but also angry because the driver who killed her daughter was still driving on the streets, even though he had recently been arrested for another hit and run accident. Mrs. Lightner started an organization called Mothers Against Drunk Driving (MADD) as a means to support those affected by drunk driving, prevent underage drinking and push for stricter laws involving drunk drivers. Instead of using her anger for revenge, she used it for reform. Her anger was not a selfish anger, but righteous anger.

In 1 Samuel 20, Jonathan showed righteous anger in a confrontation with his father King Saul about Jonathan's best friend, David. Saul told Jonathan that David should die. Jonathan defended David by saying, "Why should he be killed? What has he done?" (v. 32).

"Then Saul cast a spear at him to kill him, by which Jonathan knew that it was determined by his father to kill David. So Jonathan rose from the table in fierce anger, and ate no food the second day of the month, for he was grieved for David, because his father had treated him shamefully" (1 Samuel 20:33-34). Jonathan could have been angry at the way his father had treated him, but he was more angry by Saul's treatment of David. Jonathan did not have a self-motivated anger, but a righteous anger. His first reaction was not to retaliate against Saul, but to help David. He secretly warned David of Saul's intention, and after a tearful goodbye David escaped from Saul's wrath (vv. 35-42).

## Even Jesus Was Angry

Even Jesus got angry at times. One instance of His anger is found in Mark 3, when the Pharisees watched Jesus carefully to see if He would heal a man with a withered hand on the Sabbath Day. "And when [Jesus] had looked around at them with anger, being grieved by the hardness of their hearts, He said to the man, 'Stretch out your hand,' And he stretched it out, and his hand was restored as whole as the other" (Mark 3:5). Jesus was angered by the Pharisees' lack of compassion. Rather than argue with the Pharisees, His response was to heal the man.

Some people point to the story of Jesus clearing the temple as an example of Jesus' anger. This actually happened on two different occasions. We read the account of Jesus clearing the temple at the beginning of His ministry in John 2:14-18. John records that the disciples remembered that it was written, "Zeal for Your house has eaten Me up." Jesus used the situation to teach the people that buying and selling goods in God's holy temple was not acceptable. He also fulfilled the prophecy in Psalm 69:9.

Matthew, Mark and Luke tell the account of Jesus clearing the temple near the end of His ministry, only a few days before His arrest and crucifixion. Mark's gospel gave an interesting detail that the other gospel writers left out. Mark 11:11 says, "And Jesus went into Jerusalem and into the temple. So when He had looked around at all things, as the hour was already late, He went out to Bethany with the twelve."

The next day, Jesus went into the temple and drove out the buyers and sellers. Jesus did not suddenly lose control of His temper and start to rant and rave. He came into the temple the day before, saw what needed to be done, and came back the next day when more people would be there. "Then He taught, saying to them, 'Is it not written, "My house shall be called a house of prayer for all nations"? But you have made it a "den of thieves"'" (Mark 11:17). It was a well-planned teachable moment by the Master Teacher.

## The Anger of the Lord

Throughout the Old Testament are verses that refer to the "anger of the Lord." From the time of the wilderness wanderings with Moses to the conquering of the land under Joshua, from the period of the Judges to the time of the kings and prophets, there were many times when the anger of the Lord was aroused against His people. God told them time and time again to obey His commandments and forsake other gods. Because He was a holy and just God, He could not allow sin to go unpunished.

God's anger was sometimes compared to fire. The prophet wrote in Isaiah 30:27, "Behold, the name of the LORD comes from afar, burning with His anger, and His burden is heavy; His lips are full of indignation, and His tongue like a devouring fire." The image of fire was a symbol of judgment. Paul told the Thessalonians concerning the final judgment that the Lord Jesus would come "in flaming fire taking vengeance on those who do not know God, and on those who do not obey the gospel of our Lord Jesus Christ" (2 Thessalonians 1:8).

Although God gets angry at the disobedience of His people, He does not hold grudges. David wrote in Psalm 103:8-9: "The LORD is merciful and gracious, slow to anger and abounding in mercy. He will not always strive with us, nor will He keep His anger forever." Some people can get angry at someone and stay angry for years. I know two sisters who live in the same city but have not seen or spoken to each other for over 20 years. Although neither of them can remember what the original argument was about, they have both chosen to hold a permanent grudge. Our anger should be like the anger of the Lord. David said, in Psalm 30:5, "For His anger is but for a moment, His favor is for life."

## How to Control Anger

• **Admit You Are Angry**. Dr. Meier gave some excellent advice on dealing with anger in his aforementioned book. He said the first thing to do is to admit you are angry. People often say, "I'm not angry, I'm just frustrated," or "I'm just irritated." The truth is frustration and irritation are forms of anger. Don't pretend you are not angry, when you really are.

• **Adjust Your Attitude**. As God asked Cain, ask yourself, "Why am I angry?" As God asked Jonah, ask yourself, "Do I have a right to be angry?" Dr. Meier wrote that most people get angry because they feel their rights have been violated. Analyze your anger by asking, "Which of my rights is being violated?" Are you angry because someone took the parking place you wanted? Did you have to wait a long time at the doctor's office? If you are honest with yourself, you may find that many times you are angry because of your own selfish expectations. It may be time for an attitude adjustment.

• **Be Slow to Speak**. If your first reaction when you are angry is to blurt out angry words, you need to stop and think before you speak. Seneca, a Roman Stoic philosopher, said, "The greatest remedy for anger is delay." Take a deep breath to calm down. The old adage of counting to 10 before speaking is good advice. Lawrence J. Peter wrote, "Speak when you are angry, and you will make the best speech you will ever regret."

Solomon also had some advice on the subject. He said in Proverbs 14:29, "He who is slow to wrath has great understanding, but he who is impulsive exalts folly." Also in Proverbs 19:11, "The discretion of a man makes him slow to anger, and his glory is to overlook a transgression." James said it best in James 1:19-20, "So then, my beloved brethren, let every man be swift to hear, slow to speak, slow to wrath, for the wrath of man does not produce the righteousness of God."

• **Don't Keep Your Anger Bottled Up Inside**. You need to let your anger out. Be specific about what is bothering you. Verbalize your anger in a non-threatening way. Instead of attacking a person by saying, "You're always late. You're so selfish, you don't care if you keep people waiting," say, "When you didn't let me know you were going to be late, I felt angry, but I was also worried because I was afraid something bad had happened to you."

You could also write a letter to the person who has angered you and say whatever you want. After writing it and reading what you wrote, you might even decide to throw the letter away. Just writing out the words can be a way of venting your emotions.

• **Take a Class**. If you often feel so angry that you want to hit somebody, you might benefit from taking an Anger Management class. You can find a class in your area or take an online class.

• **Be in Control**. I saw a sign on a church marquee that said, "He who angers you controls you." You may say, "She makes me so angry!" Actually, she didn't make you angry at all. You chose to become angry. If you allow people to annoy you and cause you to be irritable, then you are letting them control you.

When you do and say things hastily in anger, you do things that you wouldn't normally do. When Moses came down from Mt. Sinai after receiving the Ten Commandments from God, he saw the people worshiping a golden calf. Exodus 32:19 gives his reaction: "So Moses' anger became hot, and he cast the tablets out of his hands and broke them at the foot of the mountain." In hasty anger, Moses broke the precious tablets God had just given him.

On another occasion, when the people complained that there was no water to drink, God told Moses to speak to the rock to receive water. Moses said to the people, "'Hear now, you rebels! Must we bring water for you out of this rock?' Then Moses lifted his hand and struck the rock twice with his rod, and water came out abundantly, and the congregation and their animals drank" (Numbers 20:10-11). In apparent anger against the people, Moses struck the rock instead of speaking to it as God had commanded. Because of his disobedience, Moses was not allowed to go into the Promised Land. In expressing anger to others, we can often end up hurting ourselves. Don't let those who anger you control you.

• **Forgive Those Who Have Offended You**. Jesus said, "But if you do not forgive men their trespasses, neither will your Father forgive your trespasses" (Matthew 6:15). However, if someone has abused you mentally or physically, it may be necessary to cut that person out of your life. You don't need to become a victim of someone else's wrath. Paul said in Romans 12:18, "If it is possible, as much as depends on you, live peaceably with all men."

Don't let bitter anger continue indefinitely. Ephesians 4:31-32 says, "Let all bitterness, wrath, anger, clamor, and evil speaking be put away from you, with all malice. And be kind to one another, tenderhearted, forgiving one another, even as God in Christ forgave you."

## Questions to Ponder

1. What are some ways in which anger can make a person cruel?
2. What are some of the characteristics of repressed anger? How can repressed anger become more dangerous than explosive anger?
3. Why was Jonah angry enough to die (Jonah 4:1-11)?
4. How did Jonathan show righteous anger (1 Samuel 20:27-42)?
5. What caused Jesus to be angry (Mark 3:1-5; John 2:14-18; Mark 11:11-17)?
6. Are you more likely to express anger by losing your temper or keeping it all inside?
7. From your experiences, what is the best way to deal with anger?

# Anger

*Anger is Danger without the D.*
*Angry people act differently.*
*Some people explode in an angry tirade*
*Of words and threats to make others afraid.*
*They may come to blows and get into a fight,*
*Or start a riot in the street at night.*
*Others get angry, but try to hide*
*The angry feelings that they keep inside.*
*You can be angry, and still not sin.*
*To overcome anger, you must begin*
*To be kind to each other, tenderhearted too,*
*And forgive others as Christ forgave you.*

# The Word on Anger

**Psalm 37:8**

"Cease from anger, and forsake wrath; do not fret – it only causes harm."

**Proverbs 15:1**

"A soft answer turns away wrath, but a harsh word stirs up anger."

**Ecclesiastes 7:9**

"Do not hasten in your spirit to be angry, for anger rests in the bosom of fools."

**James 1:19-20**

"So then, my beloved brethren, let every man be swift to hear, slow to speak, slow to wrath; for the wrath of man does not produce the righteousness of God."

Chapter 9

# The Big "I"

## *Pride*

Even though God is love, there are some things God hates. Proverbs 6:16-19 tells us seven things the Lord hates. At the top of the list is "a proud look." James wrote in James 4:6, "God resists the proud, but gives grace to the humble." The Greek word for pride in this verse means "one who shows himself above his fellow men, in honor preferring himself." Pr*i*de is a s*i*n. The trouble with Pr*i*de and s*i*n is that in the middle of both of them is a great big "I." Pride and sin come from the same source – Satan.

Ezekiel proclaimed a prophecy against the king of Tyre in Ezekiel 28. Most Bible scholars agree that this particular passage could also refer to the origin of Satan. Ezekiel wrote,

> You were in Eden, the garden of God … You were the anointed cherub who covers; I established you; you were on the holy mountain of God; you walked back and forth in the midst of fiery stones. You were perfect in your ways from the day you were created, till iniquity was found in you. … Your heart was lifted up because of your beauty. (Ezekiel 28:13-15, 17)

Isaiah used similar language in his prophecy against the king of Babylon.

> "How you are fallen from heaven, O Lucifer, son of the morning! How you are cut down to the ground, you who weakened the nations. For you have said in your heart, 'I will ascend into heaven, I will exalt my throne above the stars of God … I will ascend above the heights of the clouds, I will be like the Most High.' Yet you shall be brought down to Sheol, to the lowest depths of the Pit. (Isaiah 14:12-15)

These verses show that Satan was an angel (cherub) in heaven before the creation of the world. Not content with being an angel in the presence of God, he wanted to be "like the Most High." Because of his pride, Satan was thrown out of heaven. Later, Satan convinced Eve to eat the forbidden fruit by telling her, "For God knows that in the day you eat of it your eyes will be opened, and you will be like God, knowing good and evil" (Genesis 3:5). Satan still tempts us today by "the lust of the flesh, the lust of the eyes, and the pride of life" (1 John 2:16).

## Haughty Haman

Few people in the Bible had a prouder look than Haman, who worked for Ahasuerus, the king of Persia. "And all the king's servants who were within the king's gate bowed and paid homage to Haman, for so the king had commanded concerning him. But Mordecai would not bow or pay homage" (Esther 3:2).

When Haman saw that Mordecai, a Jew, would not bow to him, he determined to punish not only Mordecai but all the Jewish people. Haman persuaded the king to pass a decree that all the Jews would be destroyed. Esther 3:15 tells us, "The couriers went out, hastened by the king's command; and the decree was proclaimed in Shushan at the citadel. So the king and Haman sat down to drink, but the city of Shushan was perplexed."

Later the king discovered that Mordecai had intercepted a plot to kill the king, but had never been rewarded. At the very same moment, Haman came to see King Ahasuerus to suggest hanging Mordecai on the gallows he had prepared. As soon as Haman entered the room, the first question Ahasuerus asked him was, "What shall be done for the man whom the king delights to honor?" Haman's first thought was, "Whom would the king delight to honor more than me?" (Esther 6:6). He was so conceited that his first thought was of himself.

Because of his pride, Haman expected everyone, even the king, to honor and revere him. He suggested putting the honored person on the king's own horse and parading him around the city while proclaiming, "Thus shall it be done to the man whom the king delights to honor!" (Esther 6:9).

Ahasuerus liked the idea and told Haman to do everything that he had suggested – to Mordecai (Esther 6:10). Can you just imagine the look on Haman's face as he led Mordecai around the city and gave him honor? God had a unique way of humbling haughty Haman. With the help of brave Esther, Haman's plot to destroy the Jews was exposed, and he was hanged on the same gallows he had built for Mordecai. Solomon rightly said in Proverbs 16:18, "Pride goes before destruction, and a haughty spirit before a fall."

Esther 3:1 says that King Ahasuerus promoted Haman above all the other princes. Getting a promotion at work is a good thing. Anyone who has been given a position of leadership should be proud of his or her accomplishments. However, power and prestige should not lead to illusions of grandeur and superiority.

Unfortunately, pride can be prevalent even among church leaders. John addressed this problem in his third letter. He said, "I wrote to the church, but Diotrephes, who loves to have the preeminence among them, does not receive us" (3 John 9). Diotrephes wanted to have a position in the church that was given only to Jesus. "And He is the head of the body, the church, who is the beginning, the firstborn from the dead, that in all things He may have the preeminence" (Colossians 1:18).

God's plan was to have a plurality of elders to lead the church. No one person in the church should be exalted over all the other members. Peter, an elder in the church, advised his fellow elders to "shepherd the flock of God which is among you, serving as overseers, not by compulsion but willingly, not for dishonest gain, but eagerly; nor as being lords over those entrusted to you, but being examples to the flock" (1 Peter 5:2-3).

## Nebuchadnezzar's Nightmare

Nebuchadnezzar, the king of Babylon, had some strange dreams that were interpreted by Daniel. In Daniel 2, he dreamed a great image portrayed the four kingdoms that would rule during the coming centuries, leading to the establishment of Christ's church. In Daniel 4, Nebuchadnezzar's dream about a tree that was cut down turned into his worst nightmare.

Daniel wrote, "The king spoke, saying, 'Is not this great Babylon, that I have built for a royal dwelling by my mighty power and for the honor of my majesty?' … That very hour the word was fulfilled concerning Nebuchadnezzar; he was driven from men and ate grass like oxen; his body was wet with the dew of heaven till his hair had grown like eagles' feathers and his nails like birds' claws" (Daniel 4:30, 33). Nebuchadnezzar became like an animal, just as Daniel had prophesied earlier in verse 25. At a later date, when Daniel was speaking to the king's son, Belshazzar, he explained the reason that this phenomenon happened to Nebuchadnezzar: "But when his heart was lifted up, and his spirit was hardened in pride, he was deposed from his kingly throne, and they took his glory from him" (5:20).

Unlike Haman, King Nebuchadnezzar repented of his prideful attitude, and his kingdom was restored to him. He realized that all his power, riches and accomplishments were made possible because of God. In Daniel 4:37, he proclaimed, "Now, I, Nebuchadnezzar, praise and extol and honor the King of heaven, all of whose works are truth, and His ways justice. And those who walk in pride He is able to put down." The king learned the truth of Solomon's words in Proverbs 18:12: "Before destruction the heart of a man is haughty, and before honor is humility."

Nebuchadnezzar's great riches were another reason for his feelings of pride. Paul warned against this haughty attitude in 1 Timothy 6:17: "Command those who are rich in this present age not to be haughty, nor to trust in uncertain riches but in the living God, who gives us richly all things to enjoy."

## Pride and Humility

In Matthew 23, Jesus admonished the people not to be like the Pharisees because "they love the best places at feasts, the best seats in the synagogues, greetings in the marketplaces, and to be called by men, 'Rabbi, Rabbi.'" He then advised, "But he who is greatest among you shall be your servant. And whoever exalts himself will be humbled, and he who humbles himself will be exalted" (vv. 6-7, 11-12).

In Luke 8:10-14, Jesus told this parable. "Two men went up to the temple to pray, one a Pharisee and the other a tax collector. The Pharisee stood and prayed thus with himself, 'God, I thank You that I am not like other men – extortioners, unjust, adulterers, or even as this tax collector. I fast twice a week; I give tithes of all I possess.' And the tax collector, standing afar off, would not so much as raise his eyes to heaven, but beat his breast, saying, 'God, be merciful to me, a sinner!' I tell you, this man went down to his house justified rather than the other; for everyone who exalts himself will be humbled, and he who humbles himself will be exalted."

Jesus compared the attitudes of the two men. Notice how often the Pharisee said the word "I." He focused on his own virtues and accomplishments while the tax collector humbly asked for mercy. You may be saying, "I'm not like the Pharisee. I don't have a problem with pride." In a sermon that was posted on YouTube, Mark Driscoll asked these 10 questions in what he called "The Pride Test." Give yourself three points for each question you answer "yes." This is a test on which you will not want to have a high score.

1. Do you long for a lot of attention?
2. Do you become jealous or critical of people who succeed?
3. Do you always have to win?
4. Do you have a pattern of lying?
5. Do you have a hard time acknowledging you were wrong?
6. Do you have a lot of conflicts with other people?
7. Do you cut in line at the store, airport, on the freeway, etc.?
8. Do you get upset when people do not honor your achievements?
9. Do you tend to have an attitude of entitlement, rather than thanksgiving?
10. Do you honestly feel you are a good person and superior to others?

If you answered yes to four or more of those questions, you may need to work on learning to how to humble yourself. Just as Solomon said, "before honor is humility" (Proverbs 18:12), Jesus taught that greatness is seen in a humble servant attitude. When the disciples asked Him who was the greatest in the kingdom of heaven, Jesus called a little child to Him and said, "Whoever humbles himself as this little child is the greatest in the kingdom of heaven" (Matthew 18:1-4).

## "Humility and How I Achieved It"

Years ago I was talking to a young Christian about humility. "Oh, I'm a very humble person," he assured me. "In fact, I think I'm the most humble person in the whole congregation." Obviously, that young man had a lot to learn about humility. Warren Wiersbe wrote, "Humility is that grace that, when you know you have it, you have lost it" (73).

I once had a friend who would jokingly say that he had written a book called *Humility and How I Achieved It*. Of course, humility is not an accomplishment to be achieved but an attitude to be applied. We read in Philippians 2:5-11:

> Let this mind be in you which was also in Christ Jesus, who, being in the form of God, did not consider it robbery to be equal with God, but made Himself of no reputation, taking the form of a bondservant, and coming in the likeness of men. And being found in appearance as a man, He humbled Himself and became obedient to the point of death, even the death of the cross. Therefore God also has highly exalted Him and given Him the name which is above every name, that at the name of Jesus every knee should bow, of those in heaven, and of those on earth, and of those under the earth, and that every tongue should confess that Jesus Christ is Lord, to the glory of God the Father.

These verses show that Jesus not only taught in words that "he who humbles himself will be exalted" but also by His example. As Paul said, "Let this mind [or attitude] be in you, which was also in Christ Jesus."

## How to Avoid Pride

• **Put Other People First**. In his many letters to churches and individuals, Paul gave some helpful, practical advice. He told the Romans: "For I say, through the grace given to me, to everyone who is among you, not to think of himself more highly than he ought to think, but to think soberly, as God has dealt to each one a measure of faith" (Romans 12:3).

To the Philippian Christians, he wrote: "Let nothing be done through selfish ambition or conceit, but in lowliness of mind let each esteem others better than himself" (Philippians 2:3). To avoid being puffed up and full of pride, make a conscious effort to think of others rather than yourself. Look for ways to put other people's needs first. Let someone with fewer groceries than you go ahead of you in the checkout line. Have an attitude that says, "What can I do for you?" instead of "What can you do for me?" Make it a daily habit to think of the needs of others.

• **Give Someone Else the Best Seat**. Jesus also gave some good advice in Luke 14:8-10.

> When you are invited by anyone to a wedding feast, do not sit down in the best place, lest one more honorable than you be invited by him; and he who invited you and him come and say to you, "Give place to this man," and then you begin with shame to take the lowest place. But when you are invited, go and sit down in the lowest place, so that when he who invited you comes he may say to you, "Friend, go up higher." Then you will have glory in the presence of those who sit at the table with you.

Don't elbow your way to the front of the line to get the best seats at the movies, the theater, a sporting event or even worship services. I heard a supposedly true story of a couple who always sat in the same seat at church. One Sunday morning, they came to church and found some visitors sitting in their designated pew. They told the newcomers that they had taken their seats. Not surprisingly, the visitors left and never came to that congregation again. Be flexible and willing to give in when necessary, not rigid and unyielding.

• **Keep Unsolicited Advice to a Minimum.** When you are with a group of people who are talking, don't barge in and immediately start to monopolize the conversion. Listen more and talk less. Don't be quick to give unsolicited advice and tell people how to run their lives. Whenever you tell someone what to do, you are giving the impression that you are more knowledgeable and competent than they are. Give advice only when someone asks for your advice.

• **Don't Boast**. Do your best at whatever you do, but don't boast about all your accomplishments. Proverbs 27:2 advises, "Let another praise you, and not your own mouth."

• **Serve in Secret**. Follow the advice of James, who said, "Humble yourselves in the sight of the Lord, and He will lift you up" (James 4:10). Peter used similar words in 1 Peter 5:6, "Therefore humble yourselves under the mighty hand of God, that He may exalt you in due time."

Jesus taught in His Sermon on the Mount that when you do a charitable deed, "do not let your left hand know what your right hand is doing, that your charitable deed may be done in secret; and your Father who sees in secret will Himself reward you openly" (Matthew 6:3-4). Do kind deeds for people without any expectation of praise and recognition. God may not reward you right away, but He will exalt you in due time.

• **Be Willing to Do Menial Tasks**. Jesus taught His most memorable lesson on humility during His last Passover supper with His apostles. After the supper was finished, Jesus took a towel and basin of water and began to wash the disciples' feet. This was a task normally done by the lowliest servant. Then Jesus told them, "You call Me Teacher and Lord, and you say well, for so I am. If I then, your Lord and Teacher, have washed your feet, you also ought to wash one another's feet. For I have given an example, that you should do as I have done to you" (John 13:13-15). What a great example for us today. We should be willing to help others, even if it means doing an unpleasant job, like changing an adult diaper or cleaning up after someone has been sick.

• **Practice True Humility**. Paul warned the Colossian Christians about false humility.

> Let no one cheat you of your reward, taking delight in false humility and worship of angels, intruding into those things which he has not seen, vainly puffed up by his fleshly mind. ... These things indeed have an appearance of wisdom in self-imposed religion, false humility, and neglect of the body, but are of no value against the indulgence of the flesh. (Colossians 2:18, 23)

I once heard a preacher speaking about his experiences as a missionary in India. He told about a group of people who tried to show their spirituality by walking on hot coals and lying on beds of nails. One day he was about to take a picture of a man lying on a bed of nails. When the man saw the camera, he piously held up his hand to stop the preacher from taking the picture. Then, to the preacher's surprise, the man pushed a stray hair back into place, and lay back down as if to say, "Now you can take the picture." False humility is just a subtle form of pride. Notice that Paul says that a person who engages in false humility is "vainly puffed up by his fleshly mind."

True humility is simple. It basically means following Jesus' command in Matthew 7:12 that is often referred to as the Golden Rule: "Therefore, whatever you want men to do to you, do also to them, for this is the Law and the Prophets." In other words, treat people the way you would want to be treated. Don't always think of yourself, but be aware of the needs of others. Forget yourself for others, and they will never forget you.

## Questions to Ponder

1. What are some words and phrases in Ezekiel 28:12-17 and Isaiah 14:12-14 that indicate these verses could refer to the origin of Satan? Why was Satan thrown out of heaven?

2. What caused Haman to be so haughty (Esther 3:1-6)? In your experiences, have you seen people become full of pride after being promoted at work?

3. Read Esther 6:1-12 and tell how Haman was humbled. What was his reaction?

4. How did God humble King Nebuchadnezzar? What was the king's reaction (Daniel 4:30-37)?

5. Compare the differences between the Pharisee and the tax collector in Jesus' parable in Luke 18:10-14.

6. How should we treat people, according to Romans 12:3 and Philippians 2:3? Is this an easy thing to do?

7. Read Philippians 2:5-11. How did Jesus humble Himself? What are some ways we can "let this mind be in us, which was also in Christ Jesus?"

# A Proud Look

*God hates a proud look, for that look reveals*
*A heart that is haughty, and often feels*
*A sense of entitlement for self alone,*
*A person who thinks of no needs but his own.*
*He likes to boast and to hear words of praise,*
*And say the word "I" in each sentence and phrase.*
*He puffs himself up and puts others down.*
*His proud attitude makes everyone frown.*
*The remedy for pride cannot be ignored –*
*"Humble yourself in the sight of the Lord."*

# The Word on Pride

**Proverbs 16:18**

"Pride goes before destruction, and a haughty spirit before a fall."

**Proverbs 29:23**

"A man's pride will bring him low, but the humble
in spirit will retain honor."

**Philippians 2:3**

"Let nothing be done through selfish ambition or conceit,
but in lowliness of mind let each esteem others better than himself."

**James 4:6, 10**

"But He gives more grace. Therefore He says:
'God resists the proud, but gives grace to the humble.'… Humble
yourselves in the sight of the Lord, and He will lift you up."

Chapter 10

# Saying Goodbye

## *Grief*

One of my favorite poets, Emily Dickinson, wrote nearly 1,800 poems, most of which were found hidden in a desk drawer after her death in 1886. Here is a portion of one of her poems simply titled "Griefs."

> I measure every grief I meet
> With analytic eyes;
> I wonder if it weighs like mine,
> Or has an easier size.
> I wonder if they bore it long,
> Or did it just begin?
> I could not tell the date of mine,
> It feels so old a pain.
> I wonder if it hurts to live,
> And if they have to try,
> And whether, could they choose between,
> They would not rather die.

Emily Dickinson was expressing the idea that people grieve in different ways and for different periods of time. Grief can be caused by the death of a loved one, the terminal illness or life-changing injury of a loved one, or the illness or injury of oneself.

In 1969, Elisabeth Kübler-Ross outlined five stages of grief that are accepted and used by many psychologists and grief counselors today. They are not necessarily experienced in this order, but most people go through each of these stages at some point of their grieving process.

(1) Denial – The first reaction to the death of a loved one is often to deny the reality of the situation. The shock of hearing the news can cause a person to block out the words and hide from the facts. It is not unusual to hear a person say, "No, he can't be dead. This cannot be happening."

(2) Anger – The grieving person may be angry at the deceased, or he or she may express anger toward the doctor who was unable to cure the disease or even be angry at God. Sometimes anger can be irrational, causing the person to lash out at friends, family and complete strangers. Because of their vulnerability, some people feel angry when they see other people's lives going on as usual when their own lives have been permanently altered.

(3) Bargaining – Sometimes when a person knows that a loved one is about to die soon, she will try to bargain with God to postpone the inevitable. After the death, bargaining can include statements such as, "If only we had sought medical attention sooner" or "If only we had gotten a second opinion from another doctor." Such thoughts can lead to a false sense of guilt.

(4) Depression – Feelings of extreme sadness are a natural part of grief. A person may cry over anything that triggers a memory of the deceased person. Some people will want to talk about their emotions while others prefer to withdraw from others and keep their sad feelings to themselves.

(5) Acceptance – In time, most people will accept the fact that the loved one is gone and show signs of being able to go on with their lives. They will still feel sad at times, but the deep depression will eventually diminish. It could take several months or many years to reach this stage of grief.

In his book, *A Grief Observed*, C.S. Lewis wrote that "the death of a beloved is an amputation" (p. vi). When someone close to you dies, you feel as if a part of yourself has been severed. Just as it takes time for physical healing to occur after an amputation, going through the different stages of grief after the death of a loved one is necessary for emotional healing. Lewis also wrote, "I thought I could describe a *state*; make a map of sorrow. Sorrow, however, turns out to be not a state but a process" (p. 59).

## Naomi and Ruth

At the beginning of the book of Ruth, we are introduced to Naomi, her husband and her two sons. They lived in Bethlehem, but because of a famine in the land, they decided to move to Moab. Within 10 years, Naomi experienced the sorrow of losing her husband and both sons. With a heavy heart, she informed her two Moabite daughters-in-law, Ruth and Orpah, that she was going back to Bethlehem. All three of these women were grieving the loss of their husbands, and they "lifted up their voices and wept" (Ruth 1:9). Ruth and Orpah wanted to accompany Naomi back to her hometown, but Naomi told them, "No, my daughters; for it grieves me very much for your sakes that the hand of the LORD has gone out against me" (v. 13).

Naomi was sorrowful, but she also seemed to be expressing the idea that God had turned against her. She persuaded Orpah to go home to her own family, but Ruth was determined to go with Naomi. When Ruth and Naomi arrived in Bethlehem, the women of the city asked, "Is this Naomi?" (v. 19).

Naomi told them, "Do not call me Naomi; call me Mara, for the Almighty has dealt very bitterly with me. I went out full, but the LORD has brought me home again empty. Why do you call me Naomi, since the LORD has testified against me, and the Almighty has afflicted me?" (Ruth 1:20-21). Naomi's name means "pleasant," but she preferred to be called Mara, which means "bitter." She was depressed and also angry with God. She felt bitter because of her situation. In other words, she was going through the stages of grief.

Ruth was also grieving the death of her husband, but she chose to focus on caring for Naomi, rather than on her own sorrow. She worked in the field of Boaz to provide food for Naomi and herself. Later, when Naomi perceived that Boaz showed a special interest in Ruth, Naomi became a matchmaker. She said to Ruth, "My daughter, shall I not seek security for you, that it may be well with you?" (Ruth 3:1). Naomi was now able to concentrate more on helping Ruth and less on her own grief.

At the end of this beautiful love story, Ruth married Boaz and had a son, Obed, who became for Naomi, "a restorer of life and nourisher of [her] old age" (Ruth 4:15). Naomi eventually came to the acceptance stage of her grief and was able to experience love and joy once again.

## Mary and Martha

Jesus had some friends in Bethany, two sisters, Mary and Martha, and their brother, Lazarus. When Lazarus became sick, his sisters sent for Jesus to come. John tells us, "Now Jesus loved Martha and her sister and Lazarus. So, when He heard that he was sick, He stayed two more days in the place where He was" (John 11:5-6). Jesus finally went to Bethany, but by that time, Lazarus had been dead for four days (v. 39).

When Martha came to meet Jesus, the first thing she said to Him was, "Lord, if You had been here, my brother would not have died" (John 11:21). Martha may have been just expressing a fact, but there could have been some annoyance at Jesus for not coming sooner. Often when people are grieving a death, they look for someone to blame.

Even in her sorrow, Martha made some strong faith statements. After her disappointment that Jesus had not been there, she quickly added, "But even now I know that whatever You ask of God, God will give You" (John 11:22). She also said, "I know that he will rise again in the resurrection at the last day" (v. 24). There is great comfort in knowing that a loved one who has departed this life will go on to a better life. Finally, with an unwavering conviction, Martha said in verse 27, "Yes, Lord, I believe that You are the Christ, the Son of God, who is to come into the world." A strong faith is a great help and comfort to those who are grieving.

Although Mary came to see Jesus later, her first words were exactly the same as her sister's: "Lord, if You had been here, my brother would not have died" (John 11:32). Tears began to flow from her eyes. The shortest verse in the Bible, John 11:35, says, "Jesus wept." Those two little words speak volumes about the character of Jesus. He knew He would soon bring Lazarus back from the dead, but at that moment He was overcome with emotion because of the sorrow that death brought to His beloved friends. Jesus understood how Mary and Martha felt because He was also "a Man of sorrows, and acquainted with grief" (Isaiah 53:3). In a beautiful prayer to God, David wrote, "Put my tears in Your bottle; are they not in Your book?" (Psalm 56:8). No matter what pain or sorrow we are experiencing, we can be assured that Jesus cares. He sees all our tears and puts them in His bottle.

Martha said earlier that she knew her brother would rise again. Little did she know how soon that fact would occur. Jesus showed His authority over death by commanding Lazarus to "come forth" (John 11:43). To the amazement of all who were present, Lazarus did come forth from the grave. Mary and Martha's grief was quickly turned to gratitude.

## "It Is Well"

In 2 Kings, we read about a lady, known only as the Shunammite woman, who showed hospitality to Elisha the prophet. To show his gratitude for her kindness, Elisha told the woman that she would have a baby. The Shunammite woman was skeptical because she had no children and her husband was old, but she did have a baby boy the following year, just as Elisha had prophesied.

Years later, when the child was a young boy, a terrible thing happened. He became ill and died suddenly on his mother's knee (2 Kings 4:20). Surely nothing could be worse for a mother than to witness the death of her own child. I can only imagine the loss and devastation the Shunammite woman must have felt as she looked upon her lifeless son. Her first thought was to go to Elisha. She didn't even tell her husband what had happened. She asked for one of the donkeys so she could go to the "man of God." When asked why she was going, she simply answered, "It is well" (vv. 22-23).

From a distance, Elisha could see the Shunammite woman coming. He asked his servant Gehazi to run to meet her and ask her, "Is it well with you? Is it well with your husband? Is it well with the child?" Again the woman said, "It is well" (2 Kings 4:26). Elisha could see that all was not well, but that "her soul [was] in deep distress" (v. 27). By the power of God, Elisha was able to bring the boy back to life.

The sudden death of a child can be just as devastating to a father as to a mother. Tina Truelove tells the story of successful lawyer Horatio Spafford, who lived with his wife and five children in Chicago during the late 1800s. In 1870, Spafford's only son died of scarlet fever at the age of 4. The very next year, in 1871, all of Spafford's real estate investments were destroyed in the Great Chicago Fire.

After their trauma and loss, the Spafford family decided to take a vacation to Great Britain in 1873. They traveled to New York to take a ship to England, but at the last minute, a business development threatened to delay their journey. Spafford told his wife and four daughters to board the ship and go on ahead, and he would join them later. Nine days later, Spafford received news that the ship which carried his family had sunk. His wife, Anna, survived, but all four of his daughters were drowned in the ocean. Immediately, Spafford took the next ship from New York to join his grief-stricken wife. The captain of the ship showed him the location where it was believed the ship was wrecked. Spafford gazed somberly into the sea, and then went to his cabin, where he wrote these lyrics to a hymn called "It Is Well With My Soul." Perhaps the story of the Shunammite woman inspired Spafford to write this beautiful hymn in his time of deepest sorrow.

> When peace like a river attendeth my way,
> When sorrows like sea billows roll;
> Whatever my lot, Thou hast taught me to say,
> "It is well, it is well with my soul."

After the death of a child, spouse, parent or friend, it may seem that it will never again be well with your soul. In an article called "The New Normal" from the devotional guide, *Our Daily Bread*, Bill Crowder said that the greatest challenge for those suffering from grief is trying to adjust their lives to the new normal. He wrote, "It may be a new normal that no longer includes robust health, a treasured relationship or a satisfying job, or it may be living without a loved one who has been taken in death. The gravity of such losses forces us to live a different kind of life – no matter how unwelcome it may be."

One lady who was widowed expressed her feelings in this way: "There is an extra place at the table, an empty seat in the car, an empty space beside me at church, buy-one-get-one-free coupons are useless, and the life I loved is gone, except for the memories. It is an experience that is very hard to describe. There is a hole in my heart, but I know that with time, it will be easier."

After Job lost all 10 of his children at once and then suffered from a physical malady of painful boils, he cried out, "Oh, that my grief were fully weighed, and my calamity laid with it on the scales!" (Job 6:2). No one can measure the weight of a person's grief. At times, it may seem like a burden that is too hard to bear. Just remember grief is a process and every grieving person must pass through all the stages. With time, the burden will be lighter. Jesus promised in the Beatitudes, "Blessed are those who mourn, for they shall be comforted" (Matthew 5:4).

## How to Process Grief

• **Accept the Sympathy of Others Graciously**. At my father's funeral, one of my friends offered her condolences by saying, "I know exactly how you feel. My dog died last week." Her words made me smile. I was not offended because I knew it was her way of letting me know she shared my sorrow. Some people feel awkward and don't know what to say during a time of loss. Their words may not come out in the right way, but be patient with them and grateful for their concern.

If you know someone who is grieving, here are some suggestions on how to help.

(1) Don't try to think of clever things to say. Job 2:13 tells what happened when Job's friends came to comfort him in his grief. "So they sat down with him on the ground seven days and seven nights, and no one spoke a word to him, for they saw that his grief was very great." Sometimes just giving a hug or a sympathetic look can be more effective than words.

(2) Don't tell a grieving person not to cry. Weeping is a way of releasing the emotions that are welled up inside and is a natural and often necessary part of the grieving process. Paul wrote in Romans 12:15, "Rejoice with those who rejoice, and weep with those who weep."

(3) Don't give advice or predictions. Job's friends gave plenty of advice to him after his ordeal, causing him to cry out, "Miserable comforters are you all!" (Job 16:2). I know a lady who became a widow very suddenly when she was in her 40s. During her husband's visitation, as she was looking at his body in the coffin someone came up to her and said, "Don't worry, you'll find someone else." That person was

probably trying to make her feel better, but the remark only made her angry. A person who is struggling with grief does not need advice. He or she just needs to know that others care.

(4) Do call or visit as much as you can. I know another lady whose husband died, and she had many calls and visits just before and after the funeral. Many weeks later, she lamented to me that nobody called anymore. "It seems like everyone has forgotten me," she said sadly. If you have a friend who is grieving, do your best to keep in touch with her on a regular basis. Invite her to social activities. If she declines, ask again at a later date. Don't give up on her.

(5) Do share your fond memories of the deceased person with the bereaved family. Some people feel uncomfortable talking about the departed person to the family for fear it will make them sorrowful. In his book, *When Life Tumbles In*, Dr. Batsell Barrett Baxter wrote, "Quite often, it will make them just the opposite … Deep satisfaction often comes from talking about those we have loved so deeply with sympathetic, interested friends. It helps to make the loss seem less complete" (107-108).

(6) If a person is still showing signs of deep grief after a long period of time, don't suggest to them that it's time to get over it. Solomon wrote in Ecclesiastes 3:4: "A time to weep, and a time to laugh. A time to mourn, and a time to dance." The time table is not the same for each individual. Be sympathetic and don't judge.

• **Allow Time to Grieve**. If you have lost a loved one, allow yourself time to grieve. In an online article on the five stages of grief, Julie Axelrod wrote, "The best thing you can do is to allow yourself to feel the grief as it comes over you. Resisting it will only prolong the natural process of healing." You might benefit from joining a grief support group. Your local hospital or hospice may be able to help you find a support group in your area.

• **Try to Bring Something Good Out of Your Loss**. Some people set up scholarships or charity organizations in memory of the deceased person. Jerrell and Fern Hill had a son Timothy who had a dream of starting a home for troubled boys. He began to raise money for his goal when he was only 12 years old. In 1972, when Timothy was 13, he was tragically killed in a bike accident. A memorial fund was set up, and the money was used to build the Timothy Hill Children's Ranch in Riverhead, N.Y. Many other helpful organizations have been started as a memorial to a loved one who has died.

If the departed person was an organ donor, you can know that someone else has been kept alive because of your loved one's unselfish decision. Some people whose lives have been extended because of an organ donor have the opportunity to meet with the donor's family. A special bond is often created because part of the deceased person lives on in someone else.

• **Find Comfort in Bible Reading and Prayer**. Baxter quoted an anonymous poet,

> I opened the old, old Bible and looked at a page of psalms,
> Till the wintry sea of my trouble was soothed by its summer-calms;
> For the words that have helped so many, and the ages have made more dear,
> Seemed new in their power to comfort, as they brought me my word of cheer (99).

Prayer can also be a source of great comfort. As another of our beautiful hymns teaches, "What a Friend We Have in Jesus, All our sins and griefs to bear; What a privilege to carry Everything to God in prayer." Psalm 102:17 says, "He shall regard the prayer of the destitute, and shall not despise their prayer."

• **Empathize**. Comfort those who are also going through grief. No one can understand what a person is going through better than someone who has had a similar experience. Paul wrote, "Blessed be the God and Father of our Lord Jesus Christ, the Father of mercies and God of all comfort, who comforts us in all our tribulation, that we may be able to comfort those who are in any trouble, with the comfort with which we ourselves are comforted by God" (2 Corinthians 1:3).

• **Rejoice**. If the person was a faithful Christian, rejoice in knowing that you will see him again in heaven. When David's baby boy died, he said, "But now he is dead, why should I fast? Can I bring him back again? I shall go to him, but he shall not return to me" (2 Samuel 12:23). David found comfort in the knowledge that he would see his son again.

The psalmist said, "Precious in the sight of the LORD is the death of His saints" (Psalm 116:15). Paul told the Thessalonians who were concerned about those who had died, "But I do not want you to be ignorant, brethren, concerning those who have fallen asleep, lest you sorrow as those who have no hope." He then went on to tell them that when Christ comes back, the dead in Christ will rise first. Finally he told them, "Therefore comfort one another with these words" (1 Thessalonians 4:13, 16, 18).

We can truly be comforted when we realize that for a faithful Christian, death is a victory (1 Corinthians 15:54). John Milton wrote, "Death is the golden key that opens the palace of eternity."

## Questions to Ponder

1. What are the five stages of grief?
2. How did Naomi and Ruth handle their grief differently (Ruth 1:14-22)?
3. How was Naomi's grief finally lifted (Ruth 3:1; 4:13-15)?
4. What question did both Martha and Mary ask Jesus when they first saw Him after the death of their brother (John 11:21, 32)?
5. Why do you think Jesus wept although He knew He was going to raise Lazarus from the dead (John 11:33-36)?
6. What did the Shunammite woman say after the death of her son (2 Kings 4:22-26)?
7. What are some ways to comfort someone who is dealing with grief?

# Stages of Grief

*Someone whom I have loved has died. I can't believe it's true!*
*If only I could bring him back. Is there nothing I can do?*
*Some days I feel so angry that I want to scream and shout,*
*While other days, I feel so sad, my tears keep flowing out.*
*With all these jumbled feelings, will I ever find relief?*
*Oh yes, these are the stages of a normal, heart-felt grief.*
*And soon I'll feel acceptance and be ready to go on.*
*I'll thank God for the memory of my loved one who is gone.*

# The Word on Grief

**Isaiah 61:3**

"To console those who mourn in Zion, to give them beauty for ashes, the oil of joy for mourning, the garment of praise for the spirit of heaviness; that they may be called trees of righteousness, the planting of the Lord, that He may be glorified."

**Lamentations 3:32-33**

"Though He causes grief, yet He will show compassion according to the multitude of His mercies. For He does not afflict willingly, nor grieve the children of men."

**Matthew 5:4**

"Blessed are those who mourn, for they shall be comforted."

**Revelation 21:4**

"And God will wipe away every tear from their eyes; there shall be no more death, nor sorrow, nor crying. There shall be no more pain, for the former things have passed away."

Chapter 11

# "Help My Unbelief"

## *Doubt*

In a survey done by the Pew Research Center in 2007, when young Americans under the age of 30 were asked about their religious beliefs, 81 percent of them agreed with this statement – "I never doubt the existence of God." The same survey in 2009 showed that 76 percent agreed with that statement while the latest survey in 2012 yielded only 67 percent. These statistics reveal that belief in the existence of God dropped 14 points in five years among young people in America.

What has caused this shift in beliefs among our young people? One reason is our culture has tried relentlessly to ban God from our public school system. Another factor is the atheism being taught in many of our liberal state colleges and universities. It is not uncommon to hear of a college professor who will ask for a show of hands at the beginning of the semester to see who believes in God. Then he will tell those who have raised their hands that by the time the semester is over, they will have changed their views. Often the believers who try to defend their faith are mocked and scorned. Sadly, some of them become disillusioned and begin to doubt everything they have ever been taught about God and Jesus.

According to a Gallup poll conducted in 2014, 28 percent of Americans believer that the Bible is the literal Word of God, while 21 percent think the Bible is "an ancient book of fables, legends, history and moral precepts recorded by man."

This is exactly what Satan wants. As we saw in an earlier chapter, Satan's desire is to confuse people and make them doubt the Word of God just as he did in the beginning when he asked Eve, "Has God indeed said, 'You shall not eat of every tree in the garden?' " (Genesis 3:1). Satan knows that if he can make us doubt God and His Word, he will soon have us in the palm of his evil little hand. We need to resist the devil's lies and continually remind ourselves that "all Scripture is given by inspiration of God, and is profitable for doctrine, for reproof, for correction, for instruction in righteousness, that the man of God may be complete, thoroughly equipped for every good work" (2 Timothy 3:16). The Bible is just as relevant for us today as it was over 2,000 years ago.

## Questioning God

In the book of Mark, we read about a man who wanted Jesus to heal his demon-possessed son. He said to Jesus, "If You can do anything, have compassion on us and help us" (Mark 9:22).

Jesus answered, "If you can believe, all things are possible to him who believes." Some Bibles have a footnote that says the first word, "believe" is not found in the original manuscripts, and it was more likely that Jesus said, "If you can! All things are possible to him who believes!" This prompted the father to cry out with tears, "Lord, I believe; help my unbelief" (Mark 9:23-24). That seems like a contradiction in terms, but what the man meant was that although he believed, he still had some doubts that needed to be addressed.

Many of us may feel as that man did. We believe in God and in the Bible but still have occasional doubts. We may wonder if God really loves us. We wonder how the Creator of this vast universe can know each one of us personally. We wonder why so much suffering is in the world. We want answers to these important and sometimes troublesome questions.

Warren Wiersbe wrote, "There is a difference between doubt and unbelief. Doubt is a matter of the mind: we cannot understand what God is doing, or why He is doing it. Unbelief is a matter of the will: we refuse to believe God's Word and obey what he tells us to do. … Unbelief is an act of the will, while doubt is born out of a troubled mind and a broken heart" (51).

It is not wrong to question. Throughout the Bible, people questioned God. Gideon was hiding from the Midianites who were oppressing Israel when he was approached by an angel who said, "The LORD is with you, you mighty man of valor!" Gideon asked, "If the LORD is with us, why then has all this happened to us?" (Judges 6:12-13).

Habakkuk asked God, "Why do You look at those who deal treacherously, and hold Your tongue when the wicked devours a person more righteous than he?" (Habakkuk 1:13).

John the Baptist boldly proclaimed, "Behold the Lamb of God who takes away the sin of the world!" (John 1:29). But later when he was in prison, John sent a message to ask Jesus, "Are You the Coming One, or do we look for another?" (Matthew 11:3). Jesus answered, "Go and tell John the things that you see. The blind see and the lame walk; the lepers are cleansed and the deaf hear; the dead are raised up and the poor have the gospel preached to them" (vv. 4-5). Jesus didn't scold John for asking the question. He answered by showing him the evidence. Oswald Chambers said, "Doubt is not always a sign that a man is wrong. It may be a sign that he is thinking."

## Doubting Thomas

After Jesus died and rose from the dead, He appeared to all His disciples at once, except for Thomas, who was not with them at the time. When the disciples told Thomas they had seen Jesus, he replied, "Unless I see in His hands the print of the nails, and put my finger into the print of the nails, and put my hand into His side, I will not believe" (John 20:25).

A week later, Jesus stood before Thomas and showed him His hands and His side. Thomas immediately acknowledged, "My Lord and my God!" Jesus gently chided, "Thomas, because you have seen Me, you have believed. Blessed are those who have not seen and yet have believed" (John 20:28-29).

Because of this account, poor Thomas has gone down in history as "Doubting Thomas." Before we cast judgment on Thomas, let's look at Mark's account of the resurrection in Mark 16:12-14: "After that, He appeared in another form to two of them as they walked and went into the country. And they went and told it to the rest, but they did not believe them either. Later He appeared to the eleven as they sat at the table; and He rebuked their unbelief and hardness of heart, because they did not believe those who had seen Him after He had risen." So, it wasn't just Thomas who doubted. All the apostles refused to believe Jesus was resurrected until they had seen Him for themselves.

We can see another side of Thomas' character in two other scriptures. When Jesus was about to go back to Judea, even after His life had been threatened there, Thomas said, "Let us also go, that we may die with Him" (John 11:16). That statement showed a great loyalty to Jesus and a willingness to die with Him. In another passage, Jesus was speaking to His disciples just before His betrayal and crucifixion. Jesus said that He was going away and that the disciples knew the way. Thomas asked, "Lord, we do not know where You are going, and how can we know the way?" (John 14:5). Thomas wasn't disputing what Jesus said. He just wanted to know the facts. He wanted to know where Jesus was going, so he could know for sure how to find Him. Thomas' question prompted the immortal words of Jesus, "I am the way, the truth and the life. No one comes to the Father except through Me" (v. 6).

It's human nature to want evidence for believing in something. We can't believe everything we hear. It is necessary to weigh the evidence to make sure that what we believe is true. John said in 1 John 4:1 to "test the spirits, whether they are from God; because many false prophets have gone out into the world."

Many people in the name of religion have led people astray with false beliefs. Harold Camping led a campaign through his radio program and billboards to convince people that the world would end on May 21, 2011. His followers believed his prediction, and some of them quit their jobs in preparation for the end time. But Camping was wrong in his assessment, and those who believed him ended up feeling foolish.

Camping was not the first person to lead people astray, and he will definitely not be the last. With so many false teachers trying to promote their theories, it is important to do as the Bereans did in Acts 17:11. They "searched the Scriptures daily to find out whether these things were so." A person who tries to follow every new doctrine or teaching can become confused and disillusioned. James described such a person in this way, "He who doubts is like a wave of the sea driven and tossed by the wind. For let not that man suppose that he will receive anything from the Lord; he is a double-minded man, unstable in all his ways" (James 1:6-8).

Paul used similar imagery in Ephesians 4:14 when he said "that we should no longer be children, tossed to and fro and carried about with every wind of doctrine, by the trickery of men, in the cunning craftiness of deceitful plotting." A tumbleweed has no root and will roll around the desert wherever the wind takes it. A tree that is steadfastly planted will not move, no matter how much the wind may blow against it. We need to be like the tree, rooted and grounded in the Word, "steadfast, immovable, always abounding in the work of the Lord" (1 Corinthians 15:58).

## Self-Doubt

Another kind of doubt is self-doubt, which is a form of low self-esteem. Some people doubt their own ability to succeed. When Sarah heard that she would have a baby at the age of 90, she laughed and asked, "After I have grown old, shall I have pleasure, my lord being old also?" God answered, "Is anything too hard for the LORD?" (Genesis 18:12-14). In a sense, doubting ourselves is also doubting God because we are showing a lack of faith in the abilities He has given us.

Some people have self-doubt because of their youth and inexperience. God told Jeremiah, "Before I formed you in the womb I knew you; before you were born, I sanctified you; I ordained you a prophet to the nations" (Jeremiah 1:5). How amazing to realize that even before we are born, God knows what we can do and what we will accomplish in life. Jeremiah was not so sure of himself. His response was, "Ah, Lord GOD! Behold, I cannot speak, for I am a youth." But God reassured him, "Do not say, 'I am a youth,' for you shall go to all to whom I send you. ... Do not be afraid of their faces, for I am with you to deliver you" (vv. 6-8). God is still with us today, guiding us and giving us strength through every situation.

Other people have self-doubt because of the discouraging, critical comments of others. When Hezekiah was king of Judah, his servants brought him a message from the Rabshakeh of Assyria who said, "Thus says the great king, the king of Assyria, 'What confidence is this in which you trust?' " (2 Kings 18:19). The Rabshakeh taunted the people of Judah and tried to discredit and embarrass King Hezekiah saying, "Do not let Hezekiah deceive you, for he shall not be able to deliver you from [the king of Assyria's] hand" (v. 29). When Hezekiah heard this, he "tore his clothes, covered himself with sackcloth, and went into the house of the LORD" (19:1).

After consulting the prophet Isaiah and being reassured by God that he need not be afraid, Hezekiah got a threatening letter from Assyria trying to frighten him into surrendering. We read in 2 Kings 19:14-15:

> "And Hezekiah received the letter from the hand of the messengers, and read it; and Hezekiah went up to the house of the LORD, and spread it before the LORD. Then Hezekiah prayed before the LORD, and said: 'Oh LORD God of Israel, the One who dwells between the cherubim, You are God, You alone, of all the kingdoms of the earth. You have made heaven and earth.' "

Although the Assyrians tried to shake Hezekiah's confidence in God and in his own ability to lead the Israelites, he refused to give in to their demands. He found encouragement from the godly counsel of Isaiah and through prayer. Hezekiah's prayer showed that he had faith in the power of God in spite of the disparaging words of the enemy. When others try to shake our faith in God and ourselves, we need to do as Hezekiah did and "spread it before the LORD."

Some people have self-doubt because they feel they cannot measure up against the successes of others. In the parable of the talents, Jesus told of a master who gave five talents to one servant, two talents to another servant, and one talent to another "to each according to his own ability; and immediately he went on a journey" (Matthew 25:15). When the master returned, he found that the five-talent man and the two-talent man had invested their money and doubled what they had. The one-talent man was rebuked because he had hidden his talent in the ground.

Perhaps the one-talent man felt he would not be capable of measuring up to the success of the other two servants. He was punished by the master, not because of his inability to equal the success of his co-workers, but because of his unwillingness even to try. The master gave to each man according to his own ability. When he gave the one talent to his servant, he didn't expect him to do as well as the others, but he did expect him to do the best with what he had.

Last, some people have self-doubt because of a physical disability. Paul had an impediment that he referred to as his "thorn in the flesh" (2 Corinthians 12:7). No one knows exactly what the thorn in the flesh was, but some scholars have speculated that it could be a chronic eye problem or some other physical malady. Paul said that he pleaded with the Lord three times that it might depart from him, but the Lord said, "My grace is sufficient for you, for My strength is made perfect in weakness" (vv. 8-9).

Paul then went on to say that he took pleasure in his infirmities "for when I am weak, then I am strong" (v. 10). Many other people have accomplished great things despite physical disabilities. Helen Keller was blind and deaf, but she earned a college degree and became an author and lecturer. Beethoven wrote some of the greatest music ever written, even when he was almost completely deaf.

Nick Vujicic is an author and motivational speaker who has traveled worldwide despite the fact that he was born with no arms and no legs. His website declares his motto – "Life Without Limbs: From No Limbs to No Limits." You can type his name into a search site on your computer and see some amazing videos of his positive and enthusiastic message of hope. Despite being born into such adverse circumstances, Vujicic chose to use his physical imperfection to encourage others.

Paul also had his share of adverse circumstances. He gave a list in 2 Corinthians 11:23-28 that included imprisonment, beatings, shipwreck, perilous journeys, sleeplessness, hunger and thirst. He could have become discouraged by these trials and given up his faith. Instead he wrote in 2 Corinthians 4:8-9: "We are hard-pressed on every side, yet not crushed; we are perplexed, but not in despair; persecuted, but not forsaken; struck down, but not destroyed."

Discouragement does not have to result in doubt. God has given us "all things that pertain to life and godliness" (2 Peter 1:3). We never need to doubt God's existence or His Word; neither do we need to doubt ourselves.

## How to Deal With Doubt

• **The Best Antidote for Doubt Is Faith**. The Bible says, "So then faith comes by hearing, and hearing by the word of God" (Romans 10:17). Our faith in God comes when we learn about Him through His Word. The writer of Hebrews says, "But without faith it is impossible to please Him, for he who comes to God must believe that He is, and that He is a rewarder of those who diligently seek Him" (Hebrews 11:6). It is not enough to just believe in God, for "even the demons believe – and tremble!" (James 2:19). You must not just believe that God exists, but you must also diligently seek Him.

Jesus' disciples once requested, "Increase our faith" (Luke 17:5). Jesus told them that if they had faith as a mustard seed they would be able to accomplish great things. He explained in Matthew 13:32 that the mustard seed is "the least of all the seeds; but when it is grown it is greater than the herbs and becomes a tree, so that the birds of the air come and nest in its branches." Faith starts out small, but it grows as you study God's Word and learn to love and trust Him more.

Jesus told His disciples in Mark 11:22-23, "Have faith in God. For assuredly, I say to you, whoever says to this mountain, 'Be removed and be cast into the sea,' and does not doubt in his heart, but believes that those things he says will be done, he will have whatever he says." John McArthur wrote in *The McArthur Study Bible* that Jesus' reference to the mountain was a common metaphor in Jewish literature to describe the ability to solve difficult problems. Jesus was encouraging His disciples to believe and trust in God to help them with any difficult circumstances.

Peter said that you should add to your faith virtue, which is moral excellence. Next you should add knowledge. As you learn more, you will be able to add self-control, perseverance, godliness, brotherly kindness and love (2 Peter 1:5-7). Faith is the foundation on which you can build your Christian life. It is not a passive faith, but a working faith, for "faith without works is dead" (James 2:26). Once your faith grows and matures, you will be able to overcome doubts through Bible study and prayer. "And this is the victory that has overcome the world – our faith" (1 John 5:4).

• **Give a Ready Answer**. If you know people at school or work who are trying to undermine your belief in God, you need to be ready to answer their claims. Peter said to "always be ready to give a defense to everyone who asks you a reason for the hope that is in you, with meekness and fear" (1 Peter 3:15). You can find some excellent books, magazines and videos on Christian evidences that will give you the information you need to refute such theories as evolution, atheism and many other false teachings. For some amazing evidence of the reliability of the Scriptures, I would recommend a video by Kyle Butt and Eric Lyons called *Is the Bible From God?* The two presenters prove the inerrancy of the Bible through science, prophecy and archeology and also refute so-called Bible contradictions.

It's good to discuss opinions on such important matters because it helps to strengthen your faith and increase your knowledge. However, if you have friends who frequently belittle you and try to turn you away from your beliefs, then it may be time to find some new friends. A real friend will respect you and your opinions, even if she does not agree with them.

• **Keep Working**. If you have self-doubt because of negative, discouraging remarks from others, don't despair. Nehemiah wrote of his experiences in helping to rebuild the walls of Jerusalem after the Jews came back from spending 70 years of captivity in Babylon. Two men, Sanballat and Tobiah, mocked the Jews, trying to discourage them from completing their task. Despite their verbal attacks, the Jews continued to build the wall because "the people had a mind to work" (Nehemiah 4:6).

When Sanballat and Tobiah saw that the wall was being built despite their taunts, they tried a different tactic. They sent a message to Nehemiah asking him to meet with them, but Nehemiah refused saying, "I am doing a great work, so that I cannot come down. Why should the work cease while I leave and go down to you?" (Nehemiah 6:3). If you are doing a great work, whether at your job, at school or in a voluntary position, don't allow others to discourage or intimidate you into becoming a quitter. Like Nehemiah and his people, keep working on doing the right thing.

• **You Are Important to the Body**. If you have self-doubt because of a physical disability or feelings of inadequacy, remember that you are just as important as anyone else. Don't compare yourself with others.

The Bible says that the church is a body, and we are all members, but we have different functions. Paul explained, "But now indeed there are many members, yet one body. And the eye cannot say to the hand, 'I have no need of you,' nor again the head to the feet, 'I have no need of you.' No, much rather, those members of the body which seem to be weaker are necessary" (1 Corinthians 12:20-22). He also said in Ephesians 4:16 that "the whole body, joined and knit together by what every joint supplies, according to the effective working by which every part does its share, causes growth of the body for the edifying of itself in love." Realize that you are an important part of the body, and do your share in whatever capacity you are able.

It has been said that many people believe their doubts and doubt their beliefs. We don't have to live a life full of doubts and uncertainties about God or our own abilities. Remember what Jesus said to the man with the demon-possessed son: "All things are possible to him who believes" (Mark 9:23). Feed your faith, and your doubts will starve to death.

## Questions to Ponder

1. What are some things that can cause us to have doubts about God, the Bible or ourselves?

2. What do you think the man in Mark 9:24 meant when he said, "Lord, I believe; Help my unbelief"?

3. Is it wrong to question God? What were some questions asked by Gideon (Judges 6:13)? Habakkuk (Habakkuk 1:1-3, 13-17)? John the Baptist (Matthew 11:2-3)?

4. Why is Thomas called "Doubting Thomas" (John 20:24-29)? What do John 11:16 and John 14:5 reveal about Thomas?

5. In what ways can we be "like a wave of the sea, driven and tossed by the wind" (James 1:6)? How can we stay grounded?

6. What did Hezekiah do when he was given a discouraging letter from the king of Assyria (2 Kings 19:14-15)?

7. What are some other ways to deal with self-doubt?

# Lord, I Believe!

*I believe in God and in Jesus, His Son,*
*but sometimes my heart is in doubt.*
*I wonder why people suffer so much, and what life is all about.*
*I feel like the father whose son was hurt,*
*and in his frustration and grief,*
*He cried out to Jesus, "Lord, I believe! Help my unbelief!"*
*I don't want to be like the unstable man,*
*tossed about like a wave of the sea.*
*I want a faith that is grounded and strong,*
*like a steadfast, immovable tree.*
*So I'll study God's Word and defend my faith,*
*even when taunts are hurled,*
*For I know that faith is the victory that overcomes the world.*

# The Word on Doubt

**Mark 9:23**

"If you can believe, all things are possible to him who believes."

**Luke 24:38**

"And He said to them, 'Why are you troubled?
And why do doubts arise in your hearts?' "

**John 20:29**

"Jesus said to him, 'Thomas, because you have seen Me,
you have believed. Blessed are those who have not seen
and yet have believed.' "

**James 1:6-8**

"But let him ask in faith, with no doubting, for he who doubts
is like a wave of the sea driven and tossed by the wind.
For let not that man suppose he will receive anything from the Lord;
he is a double-minded mind, unstable in all his ways."

Chapter 12

# Be Anxious for Nothing

## *Worry*

For a full two weeks in 1988, the number one song on the Billboard Hot 100 chart was a song by Bobby McFerrin called, "Don't Worry, Be Happy." That's good advice for all of us. Excessive worrying can lead to high blood pressure, ulcers and even heart attacks.

Some people will say, "I'm not worried, I'm just concerned." It's natural to be concerned about certain people and situations. Paul confided about "what comes upon me daily: my deep concern for all the churches" (2 Corinthians 11:28). However, there is a big difference between worry and concern. One definition of worry is "to torment oneself with or suffer from disturbing thoughts."

What are some things that people worry about? In an online article Denise Lammi, shared the story of a woman who decided to keep track of everything that worried her. She discovered that:

- 40 percent of things she worried about were things that would never happen,
- 30 percent were about things that had already happened and could not be changed,
- 12 percent were about other people's opinions,
- 10 percent were needless health worries,
- 8 percent were real, legitimate worries.

Assuming these statistics are typical, 92 percent of the things people worry about are unnecessary. Jesus preached to people about worry in His Sermon on the Mount. He said in Matthew 6:25, "Therefore I say to you, do not worry about your life." The Revised Standard Version says, "Do not be anxious about your life" while the King James Version renders, "Take no thought for your life." Worrying is really just taking thought of all the bad things that could happen or did happen. Thinking too much about such things leads to an anxious mind.

Jesus continued, "Is not life more than food and the body more than clothing? Look at the birds of the air, for they neither sow nor reap nor gather into barns; yet your heavenly Father feeds them. Are you not of more value than they?" (Matthew 6:25-26). That reminds me of a poem written in 1859 by Elizabeth Cheney called "Overheard in an Orchard."

Said the robin to the sparrow, "I would really like to know
Why those anxious human beings rush around and worry so."
Said the sparrow to the robin, "Friend, I think that it must be
That they have no Heavenly Father such as cares for you and me."

## The God Who Sees

Most parents would agree that one of the things we worry about most is our children. This was certainly true during Bible times too. When Sarah couldn't have a baby, she gave her Egyptian servant Hagar to Abraham to raise up an heir for him. Once Hagar became pregnant, "her mistress became despised in her eyes" (Genesis 16:4). The tension between the two women became so great that Hagar ran away. The angel of the Lord found Hagar by a spring of water in the wilderness. He told her to return to her mistress and submit to her. He also told her that she would have a son named Ishmael. Hagar called the name of the Lord who spoke to her, "You-Are-the-God-Who-Sees" (v. 13).

Just as the angel promised, Hagar gave birth to her son, Ishmael. Years later, when Ishmael was 14-years-old, Sarah gave birth to her son, Isaac. Soon after Isaac was weaned, Sarah saw Ishmael scoffing at him. Sarah demanded, "Cast out this bondwoman and her son, for the son of this bondwoman will not be heir with my son, namely with Isaac" (Genesis 21:10).

Once again, Hagar was in the wilderness, but this time she was not near a spring. In fact, there was no water at all, and Hagar had only one skin of water. She was understandably worried about her son. When the water was used up, she said, "Let me not see the death of the boy" (Genesis 21:16). Then she lifted up her eyes and wept. But just as Hagar had discovered years before when she was carrying Ishmael in her womb, God was still "the God who sees." He sent an angel who asked, "What ails you, Hagar? Fear not, for God has heard the voice of the lad where he is." God provided water for Ishmael and promised Hagar that He would make Ishmael a great nation (Genesis 21:17-19).

Abraham had a similar experience many years later when Isaac was older. Abraham was told to offer his beloved son as a sacrifice. Just as he was about to plunge the knife into Isaac's heart, an angel stopped him. Then Abraham saw a ram in the bushes that he was able to offer as a sacrifice instead of Isaac. Abraham called the name of that place, "Jehovah Jireh," which means, "The-LORD-Will-Provide" (Genesis 22:1-14).

God is not only the God who sees, but also the God who hears our prayers. He still provides for us as Paul said, "And my God shall supply all your need according to His riches in glory by Christ Jesus" (Philippians 4:19).

## Martha and Mary

Jesus often went to visit his friends Martha and Mary. According to Luke 10:38, "Martha welcomed Him into her house." She was busily preparing a meal for her special guest, and like many women, Martha wanted everything to be perfect. While she worked to get the meal ready, Mary sat at Jesus' feet and listened to Him speak. Martha was "distracted with much serving" (v. 40). The King James Version says that she was "cumbered about much serving." The Greek word for "cumbered" means "to drag all around." While Martha was dragging around pots, dishes and utensils in the kitchen, she was also dragging around feelings of frustration and resentment. She complained to Jesus, " Lord, do you not care that my sister has left me to serve alone? Therefore tell her to help me" (v. 40).

Jesus responded, "Martha, Martha, you are worried and troubled about many things. But one thing is needed, and Mary has chosen that good part, which will not be taken away from her" (Luke 10:41-42). When Jesus said that Martha was worried about many things, He may have been speaking about more than just this one particular meal. Perhaps Martha was a perfectionist by nature. Perfectionists become anxious when things don't go exactly the way they expect them to go. Jesus was assuring His dear friend that she need not worry about serving the perfect meal. He would much rather have her presence than her presents.

Jesus was telling Martha the same thing He told the people in the Sermon on the Mount. "Therefore do not worry, saying, 'What shall we eat?' or 'What shall we drink?' or 'What shall we wear?' For after all these things the Gentiles seek. For your heavenly Father knows that you need all these things. But seek first the kingdom of God and His righteousness, and all these things shall be added to you" (Matthew 6:31-33). The key to overcoming worry is to have the right priorities. Martha wanted to serve Jesus, which was a good thing. Her only fault was that frustration with the meal took priority over fellowship with the Master. Mary chose the "good part" because she chose to spend quality time with Jesus.

Martha learned her lesson. Later, after her brother, Lazarus, was raised from the dead, Jesus was once again at the home of Martha and Mary. "There they made Him a supper; and Martha served" (John 12:2). This time she was serving the wine without the whine. She learned a great lesson from Jesus' gentle rebuke. The lesson for us today is, "Set your mind on things above, not on things on the earth" (Colossians 3:2).

## The Deceitfulness of Riches

The word "worry" is derived from an Old English word which means, "to strangle or to choke." Jesus once told a parable about the sower who sowed his seeds in different types of soil. Jesus explained, "Now these are the ones sown among thorns; they are the ones who hear the word, and the cares of this world, the deceitfulness of riches, and the desires for other things entering in choke the word, and it becomes unfruitful" (Mark 4:18-19).

Many of the things we worry about have to do with material things. In our uncertain economy, we worry about getting or keeping a job. We wonder if we will be able to pay the bills or have enough money for retirement. People with an abundance of money have a different kind of worry. They invest in expensive security systems to protect their possessions and still worry about losing their fortune. Agur, the writer of Proverbs 30, had the right idea when he said, "Give me neither poverty nor riches – feed me with the food allotted to me; lest I be full and deny You, and say, 'Who is the LORD?' or lest I be poor and steal, and profane the name of my God" (Proverbs 30:8-9).

Jesus told another parable of a rich man who worried because he didn't have enough room for his abundance of crops. He decided to tear down his barns and build bigger barns to store everything so that he could "eat, drink and be merry." But God said, "Fool! This night your soul will be required of you; then whose will those things be which you have provided?" Jesus gave the moral of the story, "So is he who lays up treasure for himself, and is not rich toward God" (Luke 12:16-21).

All the rich man's possessions were of no use to him after he died. I once heard the story of a man on his death bed who told his wife he wanted all his money put into his coffin so he could take it with him. After he died, his wife told one of her friends about his request. Just before the funeral, the friend was surprised to see the woman discreetly put an envelope in her husband's coffin. Afterward, the friend asked, "Did you really do what your husband asked?" The woman replied, "Yes, I wrote him a check!" That shows the futility of riches for someone who has died.

Jesus taught, "Do not lay up for yourselves treasures on earth, where moth and rust destroy and where thieves break in and steal; but lay up for yourselves treasures in heaven, where neither moth nor rust destroy and where thieves do not break in and steal. For where your treasure is, there your heart will be also" (Matthew 6:19-21). It is not wrong to have possessions, but we should never let our possessions possess us.

## Back to the Future

We sometimes worry about bad things that might happen in the future. Jesus said in Matthew 6:34, "Therefore do not worry about tomorrow, for tomorrow will worry about its own things. Sufficient for the day is its own trouble." In other words, live one day at a time. James wrote:

> Come now, you who say, "Today or tomorrow we will go to such and such a city, spend a year there, buy and sell, and make a profit"; whereas you do not know what will happen tomorrow. For what is your life? It is even a vapor that appears for a little while and then vanishes away. Instead you ought to say, "If the Lord wills, we shall do this or that." (James 4:13-15)

Someone once wisely said, "Yesterday is gone and tomorrow is not promised. Today is all we have. It is a gift. That's why it is called the present."

We have seen in this chapter that Jesus said "Do not worry" three times in the Sermon on the Mount (Matthew 6:25, 31, 34). He was not making a suggestion. He was giving a direct command. If Jesus has commanded us not to worry, the logical conclusion is that worry is a sin. In order to obey the commandments of Jesus, we need to stop worrying and start trusting in God.

In his book, *Traveling Light*, Arthur McPhee wrote:

> So, does worry empty tomorrow of its trouble? No, rather it empties today of its strength. We will have the strength to bear troubles when they come, but it will not be through investments, pensions, elaborate schemes or nest eggs; rather, it will be through the One who gives us the water and bread of life one day at a time (77).

## How to Ward Off Worry

• **Imagine the Worst**. In his book, *How to Stop Worrying and Start Living*, Dale Carnegie gave a three-step rule to overcome worry. First, he said to ask yourself, "What is the worst that could possibly happen if I can't solve my problem?" Second, prepare yourself mentally to except the worst, if necessary. Third, calmly try to improve upon the worst, which you have already mentally prepared to accept.

• **Put Things in a Proper Perspective**. In an online article on worry, Denise Lammi quoted from Richard Carlson, author of *Don't Sweat the Small Stuff*. He suggested another question to ask yourself, "Will this matter a year from now?" If you are worried about a speech you are going to make tomorrow or a root canal you are having next week, will it really matter a year from now? By then, you will have forgotten all about it. This kind of thinking helps to put things in proper perspective.

• **Take a Deep Breath**. In a *Guideposts* newsletter, Elizabeth Peale Allen gave some good suggestions in an article titled, "Why Worry?" First, she said breathing deeply can break the chokehold of worry. In any moment of anxiety, breathing slowly and deeply can help you to relax so you can better cope with whatever situation is causing you to worry.

• **Look at Worries Objectively**. Taking your worries apart, and carefully looking at them piece by piece can make them seem less scary.

The individual components may not add up to as much as you think.

• **Live One Day at a Time**. As Jesus said in Matthew 6:34, "Sufficient for the day is its own trouble." You have enough to do and think about today. By adding tomorrow's trouble to today, you are multiplying your troubles unnecessarily. Jesus also suggested that we pray, "Give us this day our daily bread" (Matthew 6:11). By taking each day one at a time, you are dividing your troubles and multiplying your joys.

• **Relinquish Control**. David said in Psalm 55:22, "Cast your burden on the LORD, and He shall sustain you; He shall never permit the righteous to be moved." Peter also wrote, "[Cast] all your care upon Him, for He cares for you" (1 Peter 5:7). Mrs. Allen told of speaking to her friend about taking all our troubles to the Lord. Her friend reminded her that we must do more than take them. We also have to leave them there. People who take their troubles back with them don't get the peace that should be theirs to begin with.

Jesus gave this beautiful invitation in Matthew 11:28-29: "Come to Me, all you who labor and are heavy laden, and I will give you rest. Take My yoke upon you and learn from Me, for I am gentle and lowly in heart, and you will find rest for your souls." That sounds like an invitation that anyone would want to accept. Don't worry, be happy!

## Questions to Ponder

1. Why did Hagar call the Lord, "You-Are-the-God-Who-Sees" (Genesis 16:7-13)?

2. What was Martha worried and troubled about? What was the "good part" that Mary chose (Luke 10:38-42)?

3. According to Mark 4:18-19, what are some things that can choke us or cause us to worry?

4. What did God say to the rich man in Jesus' parable (Luke 12:16-21)? What does that tell us about how we should view riches?

5. Do you agree that worry is a sin? Why or why not?

6. What are some things that you tend to worry about?

7. What are some ways to relinquish control of worries?

# Worry Wart

*Some people call me a worry wart, but I don't think that's true.*
*Sometimes I worry there won't be enough when the bills*
*are coming due.*
*I think about my children whenever they are in school,*
*And worry about their safety, since bullies can be so cruel.*
*I worry about the economy, and if I can keep my job.*
*I worry about the crime rate. There are so many who kill and rob.*
*I worry about the future. I worry about the past.*
*I worry when things are going well because it might not last!*
*Well, maybe I do have a problem with anxiety and strife.*
*But then I remember Jesus said, "Don't worry about your life."*
*"But seek first the kingdom of God and all His righteousness."*
*Lord, help me to trust in You much more, so I can worry less.*

# The Word on Worry

**Matthew 6:33-34**

"But seek first the kingdom of God and His righteousness, and all these things shall be added to you. Therefore do not worry about tomorrow, for tomorrow will worry about its own things. Sufficient for the day is its own trouble."

**Luke 10:41-42**

"And Jesus answered and said to her, 'Martha, Martha, you are worried and troubled about many things. But one thing is needed, and Mary has chosen that good part, which will not be taken away from her.'"

**Philippians 4:6**

"Be anxious for nothing, but in everything by prayer and supplication, with thanksgiving, let your requests be made known to God."

Chapter 13

# Circumstances Beyond Our Control

## *Suffering*

While browsing through a catalog one day, I saw a book by Barbara Johnson called, *Pain Is Inevitable, but Misery Is Optional, So Stick a Geranium in Your Hat and Be Happy*. I haven't read the book, but I find the title quite intriguing.

It's true that pain is inevitable. Everyone suffers from physical pain at times by mishaps ranging from stubbed toes to broken bones. Others suffer daily from chronic pain caused by conditions such as migraines, arthritis, fibromyalgia, multiple sclerosis or nerve damage. Emotional pain from loneliness, depression, anger or worry can also cause suffering. In a way, this final chapter is a culmination of all the chapters in this book.

An age-old question has been, "Why is there so much suffering in the world?" There are many answers to that question. Sometimes suffering is caused by our own bad choices. After disobeying God in the Garden of Eden, Eve was told, "I will greatly multiply your sorrow and your conception; in pain you shall bring forth children" (Genesis 3:16). Ladies, whenever you are going through labor pains, remember Eve.

Throughout the Old Testament, people suffered because of bad choices. Pharaoh and the Egyptians suffered from the 10 plagues as a result of Pharaoh's refusal to let God's people go. The Israelites' rebellion during the wilderness wanderings and the idolatry during the time of the Judges and the Kings resulted in oppression, hardship, famine and cruel treatment from their enemies. Just as a parent disciplines his or her children in order to teach them obedience, God often had to use extreme measures to discipline His children. The writer of Hebrews wrote, "Now no chastening seems to be joyful for the present, but painful; nevertheless, afterward it yields the peaceable fruit of righteousness to those who have been trained by it" (Hebrews 12:11).

There are many ways that bad choices can lead to suffering. A person may get lung cancer after smoking for many years. Promiscuity can lead to AIDS or other sexually transmitted diseases. Serious car accidents are often caused by drinking or even texting while driving. However, not all suffering is caused by our own bad choices. Sometimes we suffer because of other people's behavior.

## The Weeping Prophet

Jeremiah warned God's people time and time again to repent and turn back to God from idols, but they refused to heed the warning. Jeremiah suffered both physically and mentally because of their rebellion. The following quotes from Jeremiah have caused him to be known as "The Weeping Prophet."

> Oh, that my head were waters, and my eyes a fountain of tears, that I might weep day and night for the slain of the daughter of my people! (Jeremiah 9:1)
>
> But if you will not hear it, my soul will weep in secret for your pride; my eyes will weep bitterly and run down with tears, because the LORD's flock has been taken captive. (Jeremiah 13:17)
>
> Let my eyes flow with tears night and day, and let them not cease; for the virgin daughter of my people has been broken with a mighty stroke, with a very severe blow. (Jeremiah 14:17)

Jeremiah wrote the book of Lamentations to mourn the destruction of his beloved Jerusalem. He wrote in Lamentations 3, "I am the man who has seen affliction by the rod of His wrath" (v. 1). He went on to say, "Remember my affliction and roaming, the wormwood and the gall. My soul still remembers and sinks within me" (vv. 19-20). Yet, even despite his despair, Jeremiah still expressed hope when he wrote in the very next verses, "This I recall to my mind, therefore I have hope. Through the LORD's mercies we are not consumed, because His compassions fail not. They are new every morning'; great is Your faithfulness. 'The LORD is my portion,' says my soul. Therefore, I hope in Him!" (vv. 21-24).

We only need to read the news to see the pain and suffering brought about by the actions of others. We read about domestic abuse, child abuse, armed robberies and murders. In the city where I live, drive-by shootings have become more frequent because of rival gang activity. Mass shootings at schools, workplaces or military bases seem to be on the rise. We are constantly alarmed by the threat of terrorist attacks. In spite of these occurrences, we need to remember that God is in control. Like Jeremiah, we can hope in Him.

## The Perseverance of Job

Sometimes pain and suffering occur because of circumstances beyond our control. Many people have asked, "Why do bad things happen to good people?" One person in the Old Testament who wanted an answer to that question was Job. He most likely lived either just before or during the time of Abraham. Job was blessed with much livestock and was the father of 10 adult children. On one fateful day, he lost all his possessions and all of his children. Job's response to these terrible losses was to worship God, saying, "Naked I came from my mother's womb, and naked shall I return there. The LORD gave, and the LORD has taken away; blessed be the name of the LORD" (Job 1:21).

Next, Job was struck with painful boils all over his body. His own wife advised him to "curse God and die!" (Job 2:9). Job vehemently refused to speak against God. "In all this Job did not sin with his lips" (v. 10). To add insult to injury, Job's friends came to comfort him (v. 11), but instead they advised him to repent of his sins because they thought he was being punished by God for a wrongdoing.

The book of Job records nine speeches or discourses that Job made that reveal how he dealt with his severe suffering. In his first speech,

Job was depressed and despondent. "Why did I not die at birth? Why did I not perish when I came from the womb?" (Job 3:11). In his second speech, he expressed a sense of hopelessness. "What strength do I have, that I should hope? And what is my end, that I may prolong my life? ... My days are swifter than a weaver's shuttle, and are spent without hope" (6:11; 7:6).

In his next two speeches, Job became more bold and wanted an explanation from God. "My soul loathes my life; I will give free course to my complaint, I will speak in the bitterness of my soul. I will say to God, 'Do not condemn me; show me why you contend with me'" (Job 10:1-2). Even though he questioned God, he still expressed his faith by proclaiming, "Though He slay me, yet will I trust Him. Even so, I will defend my own ways before Him" (13:15).

In another speech, Job revealed that he felt forsaken by both God and his friends. "All my close friends abhor me, and those whom I love have turned against me. ... Why do you persecute me as God does, and are not satisfied with my flesh?" (Job 19:19, 22). Still, Job had an assurance of hope when he said, "For I know that my Redeemer lives, and He shall stand at last on the earth; and after my skin is destroyed, this I know, that in my flesh I shall see God" (vv. 25-26).

In still another speech, Job wanted to argue his case with God as in a courtroom. "Oh, that I knew where I might find Him, that I might come to His seat! I would present my case before Him, and fill my mouth with arguments" (Job 23:3-4). Job realized that he was not being punished but tested, and he felt confident of the outcome. "But He knows the way that I take; When He has tested me, I shall come forth as gold" (v. 10).

Job's metaphor of being tested as gold is similar to other passages that refer to refining. Isaiah wrote, "Behold, I have refined you, but not as silver; I have tested you in the furnace of affliction" (Isaiah 48:10). Peter also used this imagery when he wrote that "you have been grieved by various trials, that the genuineness of your faith, being much more precious than gold that perishes, though it is tested by fire, may be found to praise, honor, and glory at the revelation of Jesus Christ" (1 Peter 1:6-7). Refining gold in the fire was a means of purifying and testing it to make sure it was real gold. Trials and afflictions are a way of testing our faith. On one of the walls in our house is a plaque that reads, "When God permits His children to go through the furnace, He keeps His eye on the clock and His hand on the thermostat. His loving heart knows how much and how long."

In his last and longest speech, Job held fast to his integrity. "Till I die I will not put away my integrity from me. My righteousness I hold fast, and will not let it go; my heart shall not reproach me as long as I live" (Job 27:5-6).

Finally, after all the discourses from Job and from his friends, God Himself had a few questions for Job. He began with, "Shall the one who contends with the Almighty correct Him? He who rebukes God, let him answer it" (Job 40:2). God then began to show His great power and authority through His creation. Job concluded, "I have heard of You by the hearing of the ear, but now my eye sees You. Therefore, I abhor myself, and repent in dust and ashes" (42:6). At the end of Job's tribulation, God blessed him even greater than before. He had 10 more children and twice as many animals as he had before.

James summarized Job's story when he wrote, "Indeed we count them blessed who endure. You have heard of the perseverance of Job and seen the end intended by the Lord – that the Lord is very compassionate and merciful" (James 5:11). God intended for Job's story to have a happy ending. He knew from the very beginning what the outcome would be. Although everything turned out well for Job, the reality is that Job's question of why he had to go through his trials was never answered by God.

When Job asked God, "Show me why you contend with me," he did not realize that it was Satan who was contending with him, not God. The first chapter of Job lets us eavesdrop on a conversation between God and Satan. God commended Job for his faithfulness, but Satan accused Job of believing in God only because of the blessings that he had received from Him. Satan challenged God, "But now, stretch out Your hand and touch all that he has, and he will surely curse You to Your face!" (Job 1:11). When Satan's plan to cause Job emotional suffering didn't cause him to turn against God, Satan wanted to cause physical suffering as well (2:5-7). On both occasions, God did not cause Job's suffering, but He permitted it when He accepted Satan's challenge.

In an insightful book called, *Why Us? When Bad Things Happen to God's People*, Warren Wiersbe wrote that "the key question in Job is not 'Why do the righteous suffer?' but 'Do we worship a God who is worthy of our suffering?' " (49). He also explained, "Satan's accusation cuts at the very heart of worship and virtue. Is God worthy to be loved and obeyed, even if He does not bless us materially and protect us from pain? Can God win the heart of man totally apart from His gifts? In other words, the very character of God is at stake in this struggle! ... In a very real sense, Job helped God to silence Satan and to settle it once and for all that God is worthy of our worship and service" (41-42).

As we saw before, God asked Job, "Shall the one who contends with the Almighty correct Him?" God is the Almighty, our Maker and our Master. We were created to serve Him, not the other way around. God does not owe us any explanations. Wiersbe also wrote, "When you and I hurt deeply, what we really need is not an explanation from God, but a revelation of God. We need to see how great God is. ... Things get out of proportion when we are suffering, and it takes a vision of something bigger than ourselves to get life's dimension adjusted again" (51).

## The Suffering Servant

We often read of soldiers in combat who put their lives in jeopardy to save their comrades from harm. Firefighters risk their health and safety to extinguish massive fires and search for survivors. On Sept. 11, 2001, firefighters and policemen marched into the towers of the World Trade Center to bring trapped people out before the buildings collapsed. Such people are to be commended for their courage and their willingness to suffer pain and emotional trauma in order to help others.

Isaiah gave this prophecy concerning the Suffering Servant: "But He was wounded for our transgressions, He was bruised for our iniquities; the chastisement for our peace was upon Him, and by His stripes we are healed" (Isaiah 53:5). Of course, this passage is talking about Jesus.

An elderly woman was once telling me about an operation she had without any anesthesia. In describing the pain, she said, "I know how Jesus felt when He was on the cross." I can imagine her pain was great, but I can't see how anyone can compare their pain to the suffering of Jesus. He was arrested by night and dragged before the high priest, scribes and elders who "spat in His face and beat Him; and others struck Him with the palms of their hands" (Matthew 26:67). Then He was taken before Pilate and was scourged with 39 lashes from a whip made with leather straps with pieces of broken bone or rocks with sharp edges. Then the soldiers put a crown of thorns on His head, "spat on Him, and took the reed and struck Him on the head" (27:30). Finally, they nailed His hands and feet to the cross and watched as He died a slow and agonizing death.

Jesus knew exactly what lay before Him, and He warned His disciples on several occasions that "He must go to Jerusalem, and suffer many things from the elders and chief priests and scribes, and be killed, and be raised the third day" (Matthew 16:21). After His last supper with His disciples, Jesus went to the Mount of Olives. He prayed, " 'Father, if it is Your will, take this cup from Me; nevertheless not My will, but Yours, be done.' Then an angel appeared to Him from heaven, strengthening Him. And being in agony, He prayed more earnestly. Then His sweat became like great drops of blood falling down to the ground" (Luke 22:42-44). The sweat becoming like drops of blood was an indication of intense stress and anxiety. Jesus willingly endured all the emotional and physical suffering for us. Paul wrote, "But God demonstrates His own love toward us, in that while we were still sinners, Christ died for us" (Romans 5:8).

Peter wrote his first letter to Christians who were being persecuted for their faith. He told them, "For what credit is it if, when you are beaten for your faults, you take it patiently? But when you do good and suffer, if you take it patiently, this is commendable before God. For to this you were called, because Christ also suffered for us, leaving us an example, that you should follow in His steps" (1 Peter 2:20-21).

We are fortunate that in this country we can follow Christ without fear of persecution. In other countries, such as Saudi Arabia or Iran, many Christians are being beaten or killed by radical Islamists. We may be faced with such persecution at a future time, and we must be willing to suffer for our faith, if necessary. Peter also wrote, "Yet if anyone suffers as a Christian, let him not be ashamed, but let him glorify God in this matter" (1 Peter 4:16).

Barbara Johnson was right when she wrote, "Pain is inevitable, but misery is optional." Pain and suffering are part of life, and we must deal with them to the best of our ability. We must not blame God, but trust Him to help us through whatever trials we face. A man looked with pity on a girl who had a debilitating illness with no cure. He said with a sigh, "Affliction colors everything in one's life." The girl brightly replied, "Yes, but I choose the colors."

## How to Handle Suffering

• **Follow Your Doctor's Orders.** If you suffer from chronic pain and take strong pain relievers, make sure you take your medication as directed so that you do not become addicted to pain killers. Some natural pain pills include fish oil, MSM and glucosamine. However, always check with your doctor to make sure they don't interfere with your other medications. Other natural remedies you can try are heat, ice, yoga, deep breathing and analgesic creams that contain menthol, wintergreen, peppermint or camphor oil.

• **Learn From Your Pain.** Look for things you can learn from your suffering. Even Jesus "learned obedience by the things which He suffered" (Hebrews 5:8). One day when my son was 2 years old, he was playing on the floor while I did the ironing. He kept trying to reach his hand up to touch the iron, even after I repeatedly said, "No, don't touch the iron." When my back was turned for a few seconds, I heard a cry of pain, and then saw a red mark on his chubby little finger. The good thing that came from that experience was that he never touched a hot iron again. Sometimes you have to experience pain in order to learn new things. David wrote in the Psalms, "It is good for me that I have been afflicted, that I may learn Your statutes" (Psalm 119:71).

• **See Your Suffering With the Right Perspective.** I read an article in a church bulletin by an unknown author about a woman who was complaining to her mother about all her tribulations. The mother put three pots of water on the stove to boil. Inside one of the pots she put a carrot, in the next one she put an egg, and in the last one she put some ground coffee beans. After letting them boil for about 20 minutes, the mother explained that the boiling water was adversity. The carrot went in strong, hard and unrelenting, but after being in the boiling water, it became weak. The egg was fragile with a liquid interior, but after being in the boiling water, its inside hardened. The ground coffee beans were unique in that they changed the water.

The article concluded by asking, "Which am I? Am I the carrot that seems strong, but with pain and adversity, do I wilt, become soft and lose my strength? Am I the egg with a malleable heart that changes with the heat? Does my shell look the same on the outside, but on the inside, am I bitter and tough with a stiff spirit and hardened heart? Or am I like the coffee bean? When the water gets hot, it releases its fragrance and flavor. When things get their worst, do I try to change the situation around me to make things better?"

Paul was well-acquainted with pain and adversity. He said, "And not only that, but we also glory in tribulations, knowing that tribulation produces perseverance; and perseverance, character; and character, hope" (Romans 5:3-4). Suffering of any kind is not pleasant at the time, but it is helping you to develop a stronger character. James wrote, "My brethren, count it all joy when you fall into various trials, knowing that the testing of your faith produces patience" (James 1:2-3).

• **Be Grateful for the Good.** Don't complain about your troubles, but be grateful for the good things you have. In my job as a caregiver for senior citizens, I often meet people who love to talk about their ailments. My own mother, Hazel Coble has a refreshingly different attitude. At 95 years old, she still lives by herself in her own house. Because of some pain from arthritis, she walks with a walker – slowly but surely. Whenever I talk to her, she always says, "I'm so glad I can still get around and don't have to live in a nursing home!" What a great example of a thankful heart! Like David, we should pray, "Oh Lord, my God, I will give thanks to You forever" (Psalm 30:12).

• **Look Back to Times of God's Blessings.** Asaph, one of the writers of Psalms described a time of adversity by saying, "In the day of my trouble, I sought the Lord; my hand was stretched out in the night without ceasing; my soul refused to be comforted. I remembered God, and was troubled; I complained, and my spirit was overwhelmed" (Psalm 77:2-3). Have you ever felt that way? So did Asaph, but he changed the focus of his thinking by saying, " 'This is my anguish; but I will remember the years of the right hand of the Most High.' I will remember the works of the LORD; surely I will remember Your wonders of old. I will also meditate on all Your work, and talk of all Your deeds" (vv. 10-12). Remembering how God has blessed you in the past can help you realize that the future will be better.

Asaph also expressed in Psalm 73:16-17, "When I thought how to understand this, it was too painful for me – until I went into the sanctuary of God. Then I understood their end." On the day that Job lost everything, he "fell to the ground and worshiped" (Job 1:20). Worshiping God through songs, prayers, listening to the sermon, partaking of the Lord's Supper and enjoying the fellowship of other Christians can be a great comfort in times of adversity. Annie Johnson Flint expressed beautifully the way to focus on God during trials in her poem "What God Has Promised."

God hath not promised sun without rain,
Joy without sorrow, peace without pain.
But God hath promised strength for the day,
Rest for the labor, light for the way,
Grace for the trials, help from above,
Unfailing sympathy, undying love.

• **Look Ahead to Your Future Reward.** Paul wrote, "For I consider that the sufferings of this present time are not worthy to be compared with the glory which shall be revealed in us" (Romans 8:18). Jesus said in Revelation 2:10, "Do not fear any of those things which you are about to suffer. Indeed, the devil is about to throw some of you into prison, that you may be tested, and you will have tribulation ten days. Be faithful until death, and I will give you the crown of life." What a great promise from Jesus Christ that He will give you a crown of life! If you are a faithful Christian, you can look forward to the beauty and glories of heaven.

If you are not a Christian, you need to become one by following these simple steps, which can be found in the Bible. First, you must *hear* the Word of God (Romans 10:17). Second, you must *believe* that Jesus Christ is the Son of God (Acts 8:37). Third, you must *repent* of your sins (Luke 13:3). Fourth, you must confess Jesus (Romans 10:9). Last of all, you must *be baptized* for the remission of your sins (Acts 2:38; 22:16) Once you become a Christian, you will want to "be faithful until death," just as Jesus commanded.

At the end of Revelation is another promise: "And God will wipe away every tear from their eyes; there shall be no more death, nor sorrow, nor crying. There shall be no more pain, for the former things have passed away" (Revelation 21:4). Of all the promises in the Bible, this one is the best. As the hymn writer wrote, "Heaven will surely be worth it all!"

## Questions to Ponder

1. What are some examples of suffering because our own bad choices?
2. Why is Jeremiah known as "The Weeping Prophet?" How did Jeremiah give hope to the suffering people of Israel (Lamentations 3:19-33)?
3. What was Job's first reaction to his terrible losses (Job 1:20-22)?
4. What were some of the different feelings that Job had during his time of tribulation, as revealed through his speeches?
5. How is adversity like being tested as gold or silver (Job 23:10; Psalm 66:10; Isaiah 48:10; Zechariah 13:9; Malachi 3:3; 1 Peter 1:7)?
6. What are some of the ways Jesus was a Suffering Servant (Isaiah 53:3-12)?
7. What kind of attitude should we have in the midst of trials and suffering?

# Sonnet to Suffering

*Sometimes I feel my life is filled with pain,*
*From migraines, aching bones and daily strife.*
*I wonder how I'll overcome the strain,*
*And why there is such suffering in life.*
*I think of Job with all his painful boils,*
*And how his family loss brought grief untold.*
*But even through his sorrows and turmoils,*
*He said to God, "I shall come forth as gold!"*
*I think of Jesus in Gethsemane –*
*The pleading to the Father from the Son.*
*He knew that soon He'd be in agony,*
*But still said, "Not my will, but Thine be done."*
*Lord, help me bear my suffering, and cope,*
*Because I know that in You, I have hope.*

# The Word on Suffering

**Psalm 119:71**

"It is good for me that I have been afflicted,
that I may learn Your statutes."

**Isaiah 48:10**

"Behold, I have refined you, but not as silver;
I have tested you in the furnace of affliction."

**Romans 8:18**

"For I consider that the sufferings of this present time are not worthy
to be compared with the glory which shall be revealed in us."

**1 Peter 4:15-16**

"But let none of you suffer as murderer, a thief,
an evildoer, or as a busybody in other people's matters.
Yet, if anyone suffers as a Christian, let him not be ashamed,
but let him glorify God in this matter."

# CONCLUSION

Now I need to make a confession. It took me about 12 years to write this book. I started with an idea, decided on the chapter topics and enthusiastically began to tap away on my keyboard! After writing two chapters, I put my folder of notes and ideas on the top shelf of my closet, where it lay dormant for several years. Then one day, with renewed interest, I resumed my task for a while – only to abandon the project again for another few years.

The problem was that I thought I was unqualified to write a book on this subject. I felt like a hypocrite! How could I tell others how to overcome their negative emotions and habits, when I often had no clue how to deal with my own insecurities? But I'm not the only one. Everybody has some type of emotional overload at times.

I'm not a professional counselor, and I certainly don't have all the answers, but I know Someone who does know all the answers. We can read in Hebrews 4:12, "For the Word of God is living and powerful, and sharper than any two-edged sword, piercing even to the division of soul and spirit, and of joints and marrow, and is a discerner of thoughts and intents of the heart." There is great power in God's Word.

Whenever you begin to feel overwhelmed by guilt, sin, doubt or any of the other traits mentioned in this book, go back to the chapter on that subject, paying particular attention to the Scriptures at the end of the chapter. Find one verse that you feel is most helpful, and say it over and over again until you have it memorized. Then, the next time you have that negative feeling, meditate on your memory verse until the feeling subsides.

You may feel that your anger problem, your fears or your feelings of jealousy and depression are just a part of who you are, and there is nothing you can do about it. That's what the devil wants you to think. He wants to hold you back from being all that God wants you to be, but you can break free from the devil's devices. You can do it! May God bless you as you do your best to live your life for Him.

***"Yet, in all these things,***
***we are more than conquerors***
***through Him who loved us."***

***Romans 8:37***

# WORKS CITED


## Chapter 1

McGinnis, Alan Loy. *The Friendship Factor.* (Minneapolis: Augsburg, 1979).

## Chapter 3

Albom, Mitch. *Tuesdays With Morrie.* (New York: Doubleday, 1997).

Anderson, Neil T. *The Bondage Breaker.* (Eugene: Harvest House, 1990).

"Statistics Phobia US." *Phobia Fear Release.* 4 Feb. 2014. Morpheus Institute. 15 June 2015. <www.phobia-fear-release.com/statistics-phobia-us.html.>

## Chapter 4

McDowell, Josh. *His Image, My Image.* (Amersham-on-the-Hill, Bucks, England: Scripture Press Foundation, 1985).

## Chapter 5

Farley, William P. "Jonathan Edwards and the Great Awakening." *Enrichment Journal.* 26 Aug. 2015. The General Council of the Assemblies of God. 15 June 2015. <ag.org/top/search.cfm.>

## Chapter 6

Mercola, Dr. Joseph. "New Study Shows This Vitamin Helps Prevent

Depression." *Mercola.com.* 6 Nov. 2011. Dr. Joseph Mercola. 15 June 2015. <articles.mercola.com/sites/Newsletter/NewsLetter-Archive.aspx.> Path: Nov 2011.

Mercola, Dr. Joseph. "Please Don't Visit This Type of Doctor Unless You Absolutely Have To." *Mercola.com.* 7 March 2011. Dr. Joseph Mercola. 15 June 2015. <articles.mercola.com/sites/Newsletter/NewsLetter-Archive.aspx.> Path: Mar 2011.

Murray, Dr. Bob. "Facts About Male Depression." *CreatingOptimism.com.* 2012. Creating Optimism. 15 June 2015. <creatingoptimism.com/facts-about-male-depression.>

Peale, Norman Vincent. *Thought Conditioners.* (New York: Peale Center for Christian Living, 1951, 1975, 1988).

## Chapter 8

Meier, Dr. Paul, *Don't Let the Jerks Get the Best of You.* (Nashville: Thomas Nelson, 1993).

Wiersbe, Warren. *The Bible Exposition Commentary, Volume I.* (Wheaton: Victor, 1989).

## Chapter 9

Mars Hill Church. "The Pride Test." Online video clip. *YouTube.com.* 6 Feb. 2011.

Wiersbe, Warren. *The Bible Exposition Commentary, Volume II.* (Wheaton: Victor, 1989).

## Chapter 10

Axelrod, Julie. "The Five Stages of Loss and Grief." *PsychCentral.com.* 2014. Psych Central. 15 June 2015. <psychcentral.com/lib/the-5-stages-of-loss-and-grief.>

Baxter, Batsell Barrett. *When Life Tumbles In.* (Grand Rapids: Baker, 1974).

Crowder, Bill. "The New Normal," *Our Daily Bread.* 27 Aug. 2012. Our Daily Bread Ministries. 15 June 2015. <odb.org/2012/08/27/the-new-normal.>

Dickinson, Emily. *Emily Dickinson Poems*, ed. Johanna Brownell. (Edison: Castle, 2002).

Lewis, C.S. *A Grief Observed.* (New York: Harper and Row, 1961).

Truelove, Tina. "It Is Well With My Soul, The Story Behind the Hymn." *Tinatruelove.hubpages.com.* 3 April 2015. Hubpages. 15 June 2015. <http://tinatruelove.hubpages.com/hub/It-Is-Well-With-My-Soul-The-History-Behind-The-Hymn.>

## Chapter 11

"American Value Survey." Pewresearchcenter.com. 2015. Pew Research Center. 15 June 2015. <www.people-press.org/values-questions/q41d.>

Hafiz, Yasmine. "28 Percent of Americans Believe the Bible Is the Literal Word of God," *Huffington Post Religion.* 4 June 2014. Huffington Post. 15 June 2015. <m.huffpost.com/us/entry/5446979.>

McArthur, John. *The McArthur Study Bible*, New American Standard, Updated Edition. (Thomas Nelson, 2006).

Wiersbe Warren. *Be Quoted: From A to Z With Warren W. Wiersbe.* ed. James R. Adair. (Grand Rapids: Baker, 2000).

## Chapter 12

Carnegie, Dale. *How to Stop Worrying and Start Living*. (New York: Simon and Schuster, 1944).

Lammi, Denise. "Worry." *SelfGrowth.com.* 2015. Self Growth. 15 June 2015. <www.selfgrowth.com/articles/Wojtowicz4.html.>

McPhee, Arthur. *Traveling Light*. (Grand Rapids: Zondervan, 1979).

Allen, Elizabeth Peale. "Why Worry?" *Guideposts Newsletter.* (2013).

## Chapter 13

Wiersbe, Warren. *Why Us? When Bad Things Happen to God's People*. (Leicester, England: Intervarsity, 1984).

Dish

855-509 5100

ext 11638

1-5 Joseph

1958 password

49.00 – 100. gift

69.99 118.00 2 yr / 24.

9.99

825590954446530 63

act #

1-800 Tues

1 – 555-4160 DSL #

Sat.

CPSIA information can be obtained
at www.ICGtesting.com
Printed in the USA
LVOW01s0716111115
461725LV00001B/1/P